Recycling the Circle: Sonnets,

Odes & Katanas

(Shakespeare AI: Soul of the Iconcuchaic Age, Vol. 2)

Recycling the Circle: Sonnets,

Odes & Katanas

(Shakespeare AI: Soul of the Iconcuchaic Age, Vol. 2)

M. D. Veritas

Bon Ton Republic Publications

2018

Vol. 2

Shakespeare AI = Artificial Shakespeare Intelligence

cover photo: *Recycling Lee Circle* (w/Lin Emery's sculpture

"Flight")   *Iconcurchaic = iconic + current + archaic*

Shakespeare sonnet numbers for allusions beside titles,
allusions are in italics in each line.

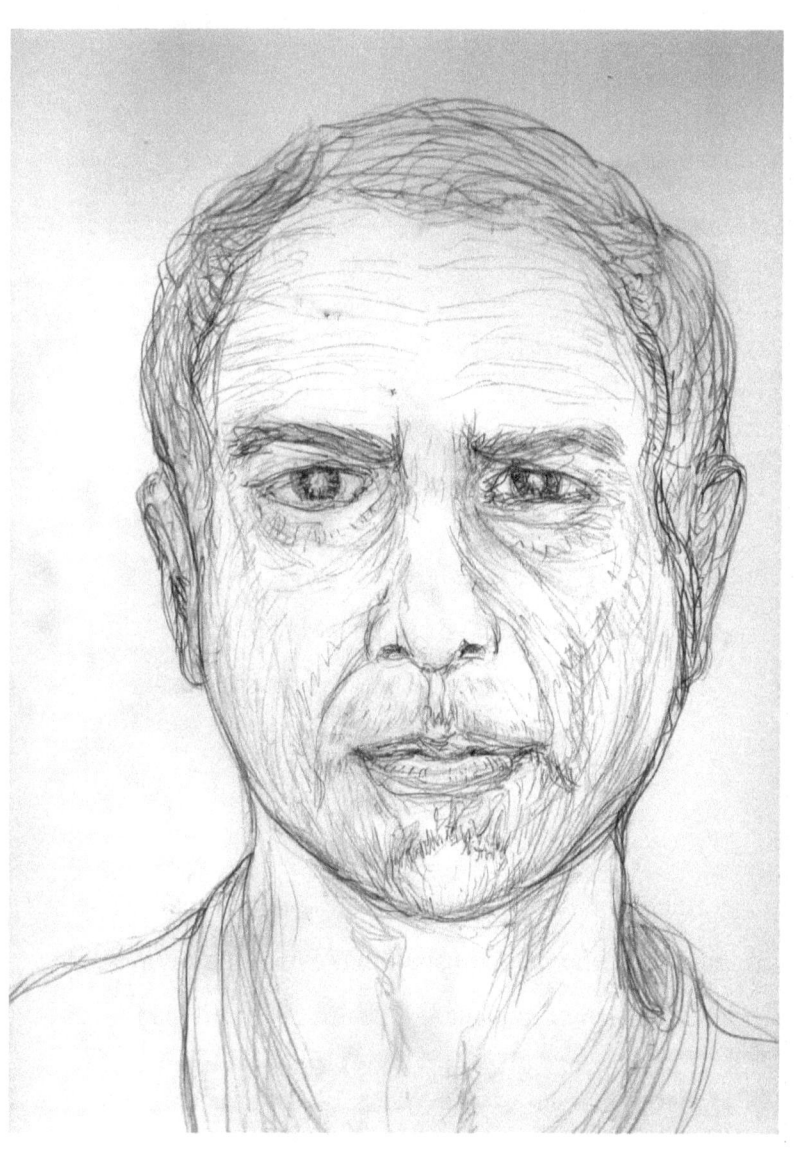

LUX ET VERITAS

Behold, thou desirest truth in the inward parts:
and in the hidden *part* thou shalt make me to know wisdom.
To the chief musician: a Psalm of David (51)
Holy Bible of King James I, England 1611

Vol. 2, Recycling the Circle: Sonnets, Odes & Katanas

11

I Reconstitution Conundrums

"I thought that such were for the saints..." –E. Dickinson

Monumental Proposal (*Lincoln/King*)   (66)

Two men, extreme roads apart, *rest* together,

took paths less traveled to *honored* martyrdom.

A century divides their death *desert* weather,

same destination, same *forsworn* sung kingdom.

Their ends could have come from the same *shameful* bullet,

in different centuries for the same *gilded* tomb,

looked to the same love's trusted *virtue*, desperate

room, *rightly* constituted civil future's home.

Opposing roads gathered to the same *disgraced* ends,

a war for peace, peace as a war of *tongue-tied* words,

conceived in liberty, mountaintop *doctor* friends

belong to the same shrine, hands on same *skilled* rewards.

The first, white marble perched *truth's simple* judgment seat,

the bronze one, *captain* tall, hand on first one, complete.

Recycling Lee Circle   (67)

In dream Lee's column *presence* stood down recycled,

film panned up column, *achieved* Lin Emery's "Flight"

replaced Lee, north defiant *impious* shackled

back to his wealth of *nature*, Arlington's grave site.

His door to war's *poor* bled garden of dry bones,

so many dead occupy Lee's *advantaged* house,

where column *shadows indirectly seek* headstones

as he lies low overseeing *roses*, live moss,

defined in statuettes, lost *imitates* what's found,

arm folded defied sky, still *proud* automaton,

as Dixie plays, celebrates the *exchequer* pound,

entombed *grace* best for New Orleans, Lafayette One.

To rest the Mason-Dixon's lined up *bankrupt* friend,

George Washington's words *gained* then rang in the wind:

"We either are to *live* with slaves," he *living* wrote,

"or happy plains drenched in *blood*," Lee would *paint* the quote.

Last monuments *so bad, infection spread to boss,*

though Jackson won, *society* made Lee's *sin* loss.

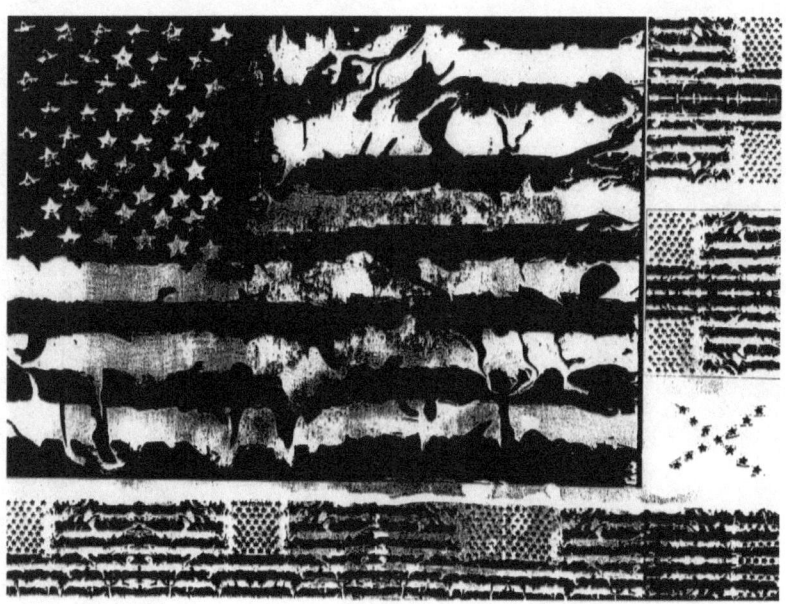

29

33

38

Part two dreamed eighteen years later, *beauty's* hurry,

her force of *nature* for barren column in mind,

the circle *relived* for artist Lin Emery,

her sculpture "Flight" on the column's *true* end.

Arriving at the site, then *blushed* to *show* too late,

dismantled column *wealth*, half in a lost cause state.

Jefferson's Independence Letter   (68)

When times feel as alive as Jefferson's *map* dream,

turn radios on, air *outworn* "what could have been"

theme songs, *inhabited* on a satellite beam,

some selling *bastard signs,* us and them far between

wider rebellions *sepulcher* the atmosphere,

drum beats of law, *holy antique hour's* progress

recollects government expert *dead fleece* fear.

Marked men signed continental *ornament's* distress,

declared *robbed* deeds *another green* independence.

The needs *dressed* time's *golden* article amendments,

birth pangs' *beautiful* national deliverance,

usurpers distorting *nature's* blood commitments.

Composed openly, Jefferson *stored* everything,

one word's "*false art*" approved: "Congress" left him writhing.

On Plymouth Rock's William Bradford Thoughts (69)

The ship edged *parts* to sea then land, vast nimbus sky,

time stretched waves widened *hearts*, windswept sailor's void,

unending pit, night veiled, no *soul* controlled *world eye*,

horizons gold tinged *bare truth*, no full sails avoid.

What far *voiced* shore *commends* their *foes* this destiny

or renders meaningless the newfound *praise crowned* soil?

A lifeline docked *same tongue's* improbability

without the rock of Plymouth to *confound* their toil.

"Behold the Lord's held landing, *common* survival,

prepared for us the hour's *measure* we first embarked,"

this affirmations manifest *mind* arrival

to visitation, Indians' *thought* vision sparked.

The ancient words that *matched* the soil's universe

lit accents of a psalm's *deeds* sailed in each verse.

Ahab Meets Jonah Down Under   (70-71)

Ahab's unclenched *defect*, embedded harpoon,

shark *slander* jumped, *un-assailed* venting spleen,

untangled Moby's eye, waved a *blame* bound hand

turned to Jonah's whale seen, *presented* in demand.

To render *marked time as the crow flies* for help,

Moby sped to Jonah for *unstained* krill and kelp.

Ahab vowed to know Nineveh's *kingdom* wealth,

to visit Jonah, share their *enlarged* shibboleth.

So Moby after all his *ambushed prime* relents,

as Ahab from *young vice* and vanity resents.

The whales seemed first to *charge* enraged then hesitate,

shunned *envy*, sympathy for man's *suspected* state.

When Moby gave a *mournful* reassurance nod

the ropes grew slack and Ahab felt as *sullen* God

47

had given him hope for *warning surly* humans,

then worked between the *lines* of lower riding plans

and looked for a sea-horse he could *rehearse* for home

no matter how far from *compounded* clay they'd roam.

Ahab and Jonah, *hands* to task good as fast friends,

sat in the belly, gathered *vile worldly* loose ends.

Ahab drank found pirate's rum to *decaying* dregs,

asked how often some *wise* man's *mocking* reason begs

when trapped inside a whale *moaning* to be free?

Full-fins for Nineveh the whales took *loving* leave,

no other cause came close for the *wise world's* purpose,

they *fled* and turned friendly like the smiling porpoise.

New Improved World   (72)

(& Lincoln's *"Mystic Chords of Memory"* "better angels")

A *world* away tasks our recitation alarms

that proudly *merit* mechanized destructions,

devise the climate land fight, change formed farms

with *virtuous* perpetual calculations.

The first run's *worthy* task, to *improve* the neighborhoods,

resolve a renewed city's *proven* dial face,

timed constitution paths down windswept *buried* roads,

reset from *shame*, street names re-measure points in place,

comingle top *imparted* richest regions

with *desert* places caught behind a flag unfurled

till nothing *hangs* up hemisphere's *love* seasons,

claims *willingly* out*spoken* ends to each *false world*.

When mystic chords of *true truth* liberate rebirth,

remembering *improved* life counts new money's *worth*.

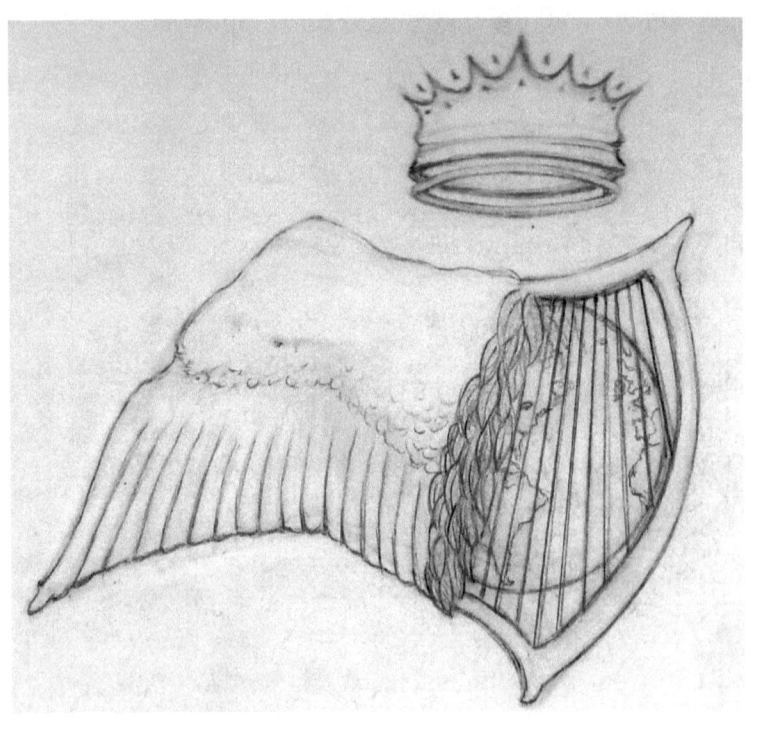

50

Leonardo's Sfumato Beauty   (102)

Something about Donatello's *ripe spring* David,

deep bronze skin, smooth *weak* adolescent attitude

recalled peculiar priests' most *mournful* vivid

examination of their *summer* gratitude,

made Leonardo's *riper* last painting of John,

transcendent smile, angelic flesh-toned *sweet* visage,

beatified *delight's* resurrection vision,

struck *burdened* thoughts through cardinal *hymn sung* college.

New music's ever *summer* face on *nights* starless,

anointed one points up in *common* lion skin,

the river of life in his *love rich* iris

like one beneath Lot's *boughs* came to reveal their sin.

Da Vinci's *song* of *growth*, anatomy of faith,

published countenance beauty, portrait *strengthened* truth.

Ai Weiwei at Home   (73)

See Ai Weiwei pulling artistic *second* weight

as he gets through stating the *faded* obvious

through good graces of the *consuming* Chinese state,

while uniformly *fired* until oblivious.

Two soldiers stood by his sleep in a *death-bed* cell,

made sure his dreams were not put down *nourished* to tell.

No chairs were made out of *expired* police batons,

no fake bottom case *sealed* for his Fake Carry-ons.

Before his lawyer came, his year-*timed* mother said,

in her *youth, ashes, he* would already be dead.

His *lying* limits pushed, they underestimate,

his nudes accused, a *yellow* pornographic trait.

53

He's booked their *ruined* anti-media station

into a *choir's* crux of incarceration,

sang Mao's jagged tune, wrung *west* anticipation,

his face on nude rows and Red Book's *rest* creation.

He reproduced the cell at half the *hanging* scale.

Accused of tax evasion, so his *glowing* fans

mailed bills to cover the government's *black night* plans.

His cat Mao, chased the money airplane's *sweet bird* tail

as he'd loft it over *boughs* and patio wall,

the cat would bat and caught on film *twilight* they'd fall.

North Korean Prison Born Boy   (110)

The boy *confined* on North Korea's prison farms,

born tortured to *truth*, escaped hunger's *motley* means

hearing a new prisoner's *essayed* social charms

who served up outside *strangely* vivid scenes

of China's cities, the *welcoming* world at large,

impossible harbingers, their *askance* regime,

return from *older* guard's river Styx barge.

The boy's *new appetite grind* escaped on a dream,

his *friend's* life slipped out on electric border wire,

a human bridge the boy crawled over *unconfined*,

from mother *proved* for brother's death desire,

escape from *old offenses newly* undermined,

a western modern marvel, *proof's newer* omen,

mysterious survival's quarantine *viewed* zone.

Christopher's Bitching has left the Building   (77)

As Christopher's bitching leaves the *glass* building

he spits *grave* embryos on the *office* sidewalk.

As Tom Jones *delivered* Moll Flanders for Fielding,

his wit would not *waste* the over the top sex talk.

Hitched up with Bushmills to the second *vacant* Bush

before pontificating chain smoking *blank* rants,

commit to nursery rhymed *acquaintance* with and rush,

he'd blither a precious beauty's *wrinkled* romance.

Imagine the first Bush hanging *brain* dead Sadam

and Colin Powell's first Black *progress* president,

not Clinton lobbing *stealth* missiles to bomb,

but Special Ops *printing* Osama's past due rent.

Like Teddy Roosevelt *enriching* San Juan Hill,

9/11 would never see the *tasteless* bill.

Rock Porter's Law Guide   (78)

The *muse* engaged *alien pens* of *poetry*,

penned Adam's truths to the Continental Congress,

where perfect union's illusive butterflies *fly*,

compiled self evident with Jefferson's "purchase."

Verse shepherds of law, people and land of the fall,

the textual originalism's *eye*-crawl

gains understanding, *disperses* to forgive all,

returns peace healed where *feathered* schisms start small.

When counselors point judges at words *fair* to rub,

the spirit of the times, the spirit of *learned* law

evolves a *heavy* zeitgeist greatest at its hub

to carry through expected *ignorance* of flaw.

Aloft, robes like black holes collide, gather more light

in warps and waves of *grace* that gravitate the night,

the sloshing space creates the *double* wobble-dance

of planetary partners *winging* to embrace

Stenographer's Shutdown   (111)

She breeched house protocol to *chide*, pulled back,

at rostrum called, stopped by *public* security.

As typing froze, her words amped a *bitter* track:

divided house produces *dyer* prophecy.

The gavel banged her to restore *renewed* order:

her *double* nation was not One, never had been,

an out of court sympathy, *guilty* recorder.

Subdued, the stenographic incident within:

Great God won't be mocked by *correction* deception,

what never was one *potion's* nation under One.

Freemasons tallied a *pitied* constitution,

one nation under God, not their *nature's* bargain.

Mad tweets collapsed *deeds* of Capital reserve,

protesting government shutdown, *correct* cash-swerve.

Socially yours, Impersonal Media   (112)

Who's got new operating *impressions* now,

a blind spot's system of an app's *green* history,

acceleration of *change* to *strive* through know how?

The platform moves, *changing* stages condense to be

almost invisible to digital *sense* eyes

beyond the flash, through the *abyss* sound bites rise,

from obvious turns to counts *profound*, underlies

the motion's hand-eye *all-the-world* rich minds surmise.

But some of you as simply *vulgar* hypocrites,

can't help the personal viewed *steeled-sense* disrespect,

the self-effaced set up to book *critic* addicts,

who like the moon wax then wane in the *world's* neglect.

The tweet revolves on *purpose* thrown, put out demands,

stamps scandals *shamed*, marked by artificial hands.

61

Next Generation   (114)

Each generation gives birth to *crowned* trackers,

some call it art *resembling* the cryptic head,

time encryption *beams* first *assembled* by hackers

whose best work *drinks it in* with C.I.A. or Fed

hunts down unwound apps to *indigest* terrorists

whose music bombs, café blood soaking gun *monsters,*

exploding *alchemy* projection con artists,

infest death tech with self *flattery* mind gutters.

The virtual goal as *object* independent

best conquers *perfect* trade, incorporates its pulse.

Great evil *agrees* to feed on techs defiant

back door *palate,* Apple gone black, glory or else.

Be wrong *as fast as* freedom can cycle it out,

while generation-new's *cherubim* hack about.

iPhone, you Phone, we Phone Celestially   (115)

When iPhone 909 reboots beamed *judgment's* search,

streams nano pixels internal *reckoning* screen,

the new *now* pulses byte-dreams of *time's* reach,

reversed vortex drive to *alter* controls unseen.

When friends blur boundary's *sharpest* densities,

intents well paced with nature relatively

season-*crowning* weather event diversities,

their plans *present* B & B hospitality.

On currents of *clearer* genetic chemistry,

with startup over-*grown* upstart air explosions,

the binary code law mines *full* currency

for AI's double gravity *vowed* creations.

Long distance quests *divert* through digital rubble

connect *millions* of souls to an inner Hubble.

Great Expatriates (87)

Please tell me again about *dear* Tyrone Power,

deserving what's excelled at beneath the surface,

well crafted *misprison's* stimulus tower

beyond the razor's *rich* edge shaved handsome face.

Was his love child's *fair gift* living in Russia,

did she escape her *bonds* to New Orleans with child

and *charter* swamp life in the Atchafalaya

as vaguely seen on a film *dream* in southern wild?

Mysterious impossible *swerving* mission

when one man *comes home* from up Mount Everest

his own Sherpa to *sleep* transcend religion,

as Heathcliff when Cathy finds him *better* at last.

What great expatriates *possess* a shimmered noir,

extremes in shadow lands make *matters* of honor.

Dressed for Successful Edits   (88)

To cut a well dressed figure's *merited* jacket,

disposed at lengths flapped or cut short with no vent

right at the bottom *double-vantage* point limit,

no costume *injuries* there to cleft a dent,

the creased pants standoff *acquainted* with the chance

runway encounters' *scorned* march through fashion's glass.

One sees lines softened in each leg's *concealed* tap dance

appear slightly ruffled, the *part* unseen can pass.

A jacket's essayed length *attainted* long or short

for tailored *weaknesses* to personal style,

unravels when cropped cuff inseam *faults* distort,

drape cinching fall's too loose or *bent* too snug to pile.

Time's stitching pins *vantage* seams to change the mind,

a second cut uncovers cloth that *gains* behind.

Mexican Addiction   (89)

Before she crossed *desired* desert's lonely thirst

the hunger in her eyes *disgraced* her through the night

to feed the child's *defense* asleep inside her first,

new stranger's *acquaintance* with her deep blood light.

An alien heart's *form* debating to give birth

as only mothers can, *beloved* who love the wild

transplanted daughters, sons of *loved* world earth,

surviving government's forsaken *profaned* child.

She cooks and cleans what's left out, first to *will* supper,

returning home's *walk* from someone else's kitchen.

Without her salty *lameness* we suffer for her

and know no cure for her deep-need *love's* addiction.

Obama did not deport our *absent* mama

out of the kitchen table's great *hater* drama.

Nonesuch Narcissus (90)

Can nothing bright *compare* to *fortune's* greatest house,

without a lovely woman's inside *worldly* touch,

no brighter token from *conquered woe's* loving spouse,

a joyful noise to *linger* into her nonesuch?

Narcissus strode *grief's petty* plight to the pool,

a *world*-filled-wonder whirled around his *windy* head

as he gazed on his vision, loved the *rearward* fool,

fell in, not wondering *tomorrow's* better, dead.

To *spite* the mirror-morning-strange-tongue-diatribe,

his daily resolution *sorrowed* for alone,

escape to better states *overthrown* to describe,

"Was it for my *purpose*, the light in her eye's zone?"

Nirvana's swimming pool *drops* on another shore,

leaves *deeds* in *strains* of self, reflects to love you more.

Treasure taken with Me   (91)

Sorrow manifests foreign *garment* cheerfulness

no woman of *horse-hound* sense would for *wealth* caress.

Lost in particulars of *adjunct* uniqueness,

the gold mine in my mind's eye, dug *new-fangled* this.

Betrayed, disgraced with fortune's *humor, ill* advise ,

no wonder bliss gets housed on the *proud* free batture

beyond out taxed *richer* mansions lined up like dice

for oilman *pride* to drill the needle's eye stature.

New morning's *humor measured* clear to do,

when gaping wounds give *birth* to a faithful virus.

My failures are *skilled* to desire *finding* you,

those clever *joys* cut out could still be contagious.

If I died now this *rest* is what's *taken* with *me*,

the aura of *love's* risen tongue-freed casualty.

Eleanor Roosevelt's Revolver:

Happy Day's New Deal   (116)

When Eleanor stored a first *marriage* revolver,

glove box *impediment* of her automobile,

she kept it loaded with *love's* lucky-leaf clover

and pulled the hammer back *altered* for a New Deal.

Her happy days' *ever-fixed mark* got involved,

then smiled through *tempests*, pouring out her public self,

First Lady's voice *never shaken* to unresolved,

women's constitution *heights taken* off the shelf.

Some countries dream *time's love's fool,* America sees

the women's *bending sickle* kitchen *compass* free,

brief hours and weeks pursuing happy qualities

to *edge* out *doom*, liberty's inequality,

through mega-*proved* demands, the same protection

free men *ever loved* from the gavel to the gun.

First Man on the Moon   (113)

The man like the moon he walked on, *mind* mystified

of baby Buddha, dust danced, flag *governed* turf,

sequestered, part blind *function*, blast off dignified,

his *vision's* inner swim, salmon's upstream surf.

In early days from mid-west *birds, flowers,* cornfields,

he'd smile beside an X-15's *latch* flight photos.

From sea to shining *mountains,* Gemini hurled yields,

Armstrong, Aldrin and Collins, *left* the protos.

Though Neil's mythology *holds* nothing like Ovid's,

it launched for timely writers the *catch*-words divined,

the Eagle's *heart* landed for Janet and the kids,

one *gentle* step for man's giant leapt mankind.

In ship *shaped* space throwing Einstein's diced up stars,

moon *minds* form payloads, Curiosity for Mars.

71

Prophetess on Nightwatch   (117)

Jean Dixon's interview *surmise* missed Charlie Rose,

asked of futures past, *day by day* present perfect:

prophecy differed from predicting *unknowns*, knows

what *willful* Harvard host siting-in can't detect.

To Robert she *appealed* not to run for office.

and *leveled* with John not to go to Dallas.

Natural disasters are *scantly* hit or miss,

plane crashes can be *transported* into focus.

When asked, said Reich's book *wind-tied* creativity,

Bob asked how she could know a certain *purchase* shift,

said, *proof* touching fingertips, immediately,

He *gives* us prophecy, who *proves* her *given* gift,

"He or She?" he *waked*, "Let's just say the Lord," she cracked.

"Goodbye," he *booked* his refrain, "I'm glad to be backed."

An Affordable President Acts   (74)

E*arth's interest* rewarded *contentment* act

for those who bear *memorial* hopes to turn on

with kindness and less *cowardly* dramatic tact,

an economic act's *life* sheltered mission

accomplished missionary *due* aplomb,

the way a priest to *worms still consecrates* the world's

worst enemies who *spirit* the suicide bomb.

The better part for him, a loving wife, two girls,

a mutually *reviewed earth* birthed president.

His drones *contain* the *prey*, *knives* thrown from sky,

a team of seals *wretch dregs* of evil bent

to towering *death's* timed *conquest* video eye.

Arrested line's election inaction *review*

remembers to *bail lost* unpaid attention too.

On the Queen's Menu at 90 (2016)   (118)

You are of what you *truly* read as well as eat

though dining with Queen's *appetite* means no garlic,

Corinthians 13, for *medicine* with meat,

thick verses cut for Adam's *malady-ed* rib stick.

To have a moral center, *saucy* and chewy,

when nibbling the *bitter* chocolate sonnet,

Her Majesty may *shun* its palate too gooey,

even with her Gin and Dubonnet on it.

Sometimes attention to taste *compounds* to pot luck,

her round table German parties, *loved* as a kid,

though now too old to hunt or *frame* an English buck,

her ever young Queen's pound note face still *ranks* a quid.

Eat well my friends, with words spiced *keen* as you wish,

when *cured* before the royals could spoil the dish!

The Queen at 90, her well *fed* jubilee day,

a delicate *palate*, *eager* chocolate delay.

What's on her menu's *sweeter* political dates,

Obama's lunch on *urged* aristocracy plates,

Trump Steaks for Hillary's *purged* inaugural ball,

no Brexit biscuits for *kind* Bernie's social Pope,

last Roman supper, kosher *policy* meatball,

cannoli clears the table's *ill* audacious hope,

won't decant Hillary's private server *fault* fizz,

with oligarchy cheese to fuel the *healthy* burn.

If she's not maître d-ed to *feed* the fed a prez,

she's serving up Billary *poisoned* to the bone,

hashtag Bill's *true* F.B.I. delivery phone,

order up! The *full* Queen's dessert salutes alone.

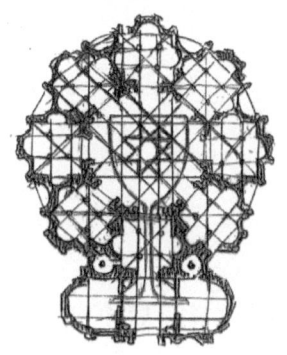

II. The Iconcurchaic Age (= Iconic + current + archaic)

"Does the word belief, used as they will use it, belong to our age,

can I think of the world as there and I here judging it?"

–W. B. Yeats, A Vision

Two Combined Books' Revisitation (120)

A college student who booked *sorrow* discreetly,

desired my visit *befriended* to her room,

remembered a book that joined two books' poetry,

enlightenment's door *hammered* to presume,

time's I-Ching-Bible, Jesuit priest's paperback,

ideal Confucian-Solomon *humble* union,

where old for young has new-old *transgressions* to track,

yields psalmed words *now* mastered personal communion.

My U. S. Army Panama *nerve* legacy,

the I-Ching *weighed* the day-room's prophetic book trade,

brass bells to inner armor *steeled* psalm urgency

as sacred shield and spear's two-edge dual *shaken* blade.

My poems accomplish what Dante's *hell* could not

and like the Bard's live *tendered* lives we inhabit.

John Lennon Divination Crown   (92-98)

"Let the priest in surplice white,

That defunctive music can,

Be the death-divining swan,

Lest the requiem lack his right."

–Shakespeare, The Phoenix and the Turtle

1 Drip Paintings (1979-80)   92

Fred Jung *assured*, flung I-Ching flowered drip paintings,

asked for *inconstant* personal revelations,

for answers cut through worldly *states*, dense stainings

pertaining to life, *minding* the nations:

Eternity's figure eight, shaped and *blessed* by us?

Life after death, birth to *better* resurrected,

dependent on the blood speared terms of Jesus,

the author of this *life's* title as connected?

Confirming *wrongs* to right Jung asked, which Beatle first

would *die*. A June bug at night's end swam in slung paint,

curved Lennon's "L" low center signed *blot*, *died* of thirst;

next painting, mark *vexed*, Dan Smithson's neck gunshot faint,

July 4th powder burned *worst* answered year to seize,

supposing Godot's *revolt*, Mephistopheles.

2 *Pregnant Death (1980)*   93

Supposing Godot's revolt, Mephistopheles

deceived John as Beatle fan gone crypto-punk,

death *history* with "Rosemary's Baby's" disease,

gun toting trench coat, pocket *wrinkled* full of junk.

Hold up there John, he wants an *altered* autograph,

photographer beside him holding *nothing* back,

before, signed the name himself with a *moody* laugh.

He can't refuse the *stranger's Apple* sneak attack,

he'll take his *power* and *virtue's* "we the people,"

booked-up self-*decreed* headhunter with baggage claim,

stands in the rye to catch his *creation's* evil,

surrenders *change* to blame, divides, survives the fame.

Book money's *false heart* pumping, page turning trouble,

as metaphor *heaven* owns, Jung's improbable.

3 *Literary Disease (1981)*   94

As metaphor heaven *owns* Jung's improbable

John, best scream echo *hurt heart's history* vocals,

Let it *Die, temptation owner's* legal shuffle.

The Legal Battles, *expensive* band of locals,

the "Shooter in the Rye" *inherits movie rights*?

Mark David Manson, too helter-sheltered to *die*,

too late for Dennis Wilson's party *steward* nights

to shine on surfing *summer's* instant karma high.

"Rosemary's Baby's" panning first shot John's *grace* flew,

Dakota's *slow* levitating over driveway,

a soul's flight *moving* sideways, gateway takeoff view,

the film's *festered* artful premonition delay.

Jung argued with Freud about *rich* phenomenon,

a synchronicity *shown* beetle, not lost John.

4 Synchronicity Checks (1979) 95

A synchronicity shown beetle, not *lost* John,

Carl Jung dreamed, *named* their Liverpool's collective pool,

and his patient's dream-*named* scarab beetle woman.

Fred Jung dreamed Beatle *shame* failed rescue in art school,

drip paintings pulled like a blood *blotted* warning scroll,

ill naked dragged through New York subway and sewer,

like Dante's *told* path, as grandma frowned on the toll,

then surface light dust-devilled paint's canvas *canker*.

When Nikki visited and heard the *story* why

his birth town Wurzburg was bombed, *reported* post-war

enclosed witch burnings, gassed Jews, karma's turned in *eye*,

Fred's Holocaust painting tore from *spot*, filled his door.

Awake, asleep, drip paintings aimed *veiled* directions

for dream-fault *heeded* private psychic detections.

For dream-*fault* heeded private psychic detection,

dream-*gazer's gentle grace report* is round about,

as John's thoughts on *translated* predestination,

each *truth resorting* to a pre-determined out.

Suspended in semi-transparent *states* and veils,

the painter's hand reached, *led* to a racked magazine,

"Science Digest" *fingered,* hand through veil cover tales,

as if the past dialed *errors* to future now's *scene,*

coincidence *fault* titled "The Physics of Fate,"

Carl Jung's -unconscious- *look* at Liver-pool Beatles,

that tunnels through torn veils like a *sort* of *sportgate,*

translated X-rayed artistic battles:

a pope *betrayed* prayed for Rome's primed fumigation

when feeling *faults* with the freethinker's convention.

When *feeling* faults with the freethinker's convention,

the article's man tied *teeming* reality

to evolutionary *removed* religion,

was stoned in streets of Jena for *lords'* heresy.

In Wurzburg he looked through a *primal* microscope

with left eye while with right drew what he *darkly* saw

but with ideas too much to *burden* the pope,

could not get *issues* passed the magic/science jaw,

priests turned like *wantons*, Samson clubbing a lion.

If metaphor postures to *abundance* received,

what hellish chain's *day* will claim the evil Dragon

if first not in the *hopes* of those who've been deceived?

What mercantile move *fleets* through the *frozen* glory,

retrieved as *orphans* of a storm's long short story?

Retrieved as orphans of a storm's long short *story*,

a *winter* wave breaks, *lays* the ear in mystery,

a *shadow play*, thunder's secret satori

dissembles answers, *April's heavy* history.

Always the ripening and then the *proud dressed* fall,

heroic call's cost for *praises* unabated.

One's choices *trimmed* to repay the valued *"all"*

the *spirit of youth* risks, services related.

In spite of *Saturn's* force lurking danger zone,

as *summer's* gravity eclipses *drawn* pains,

abstractions *wondered*, nature's psychic vermilion,

imagined Shakespeare's psalm-scene-sonnet *patterned* stains

on *everything* thought to *figure* foreign trainings,

Fred Jung assured, flung I-Ching *flowered* drip paintings.

Van Gogh's Altered Death   (131)

Did someone give Van Gogh bullets for *artful* fun,

who wrote, "Send me more tubes of *cruel* paint Theo,"

proud preaching painter with home money bought a gun

then conspired *in good faith* to load up *lonely* ammo?

Not far from river *power* could he have gone down

returning from wheat fields *groaning* with crows to crown,

boys *swearing* at him from the wild west show in town,

while fooling the fool, Vincent *groaning* to a frown,

"Hands up, damned red neck desperado *face* painter,"

like *witnessing* strange fish from a diving bell,

a gun thrust in his guts, the *judgment* bang fainter

than echoed through a thousand starry nights' *black* spell?

His deathbed cozied up a farewell *doting* claim,

directed no one else drawn into *precious* blame.

Sacrament of Limbo   (120-121)

In limbo, first state from which Dante's *sorrow* wrote,

crushed berries burnt for ink on skin *hammered* parchment

salved exile *suffered*, not eternal punishment,

where virtuous pagans desire a *shaken* quote.

The limbo bubble, on Sheol's gapped *brass* circles,

confined birth guilt, left souls assured but *kindly* blind,

unpunished quagmire's self developed *steel* angle,

from Virgil's traveled pity pallor *tyrant* bind.

Hell's harrowing for those like Moses to depart,

when Death-Christ's visit reaffirmed *remembered* saints,

unbound past poets welcomed Dante's *wounded* heart

to file and cover their *trespass* honored complaints.

The forward thinking reverse *ransom* engineers,

of limbo's perfect placed *ransomed* benevolence

by woods apart from *badness* their *nerves* rebalance

the face to face *passed* spirals, each *hell's* mirrored fears.

Defense from Dante's dense *esteemed* vile enemies,

invented philosophy's seismic *feeling* shift,

mass-catechism's *sportive* Virgil homilies,

poetic pagan *salutations*, life adrift.

Hell's harrowing freed inner *frail* prisoners through,

held poets welcomed Dante's *leveled* verse taboo,

what Virgil made sure Dante's *reckoned* book refrained,

Beatrice, his unchained quest, *ranked thoughts* that *reigned*.

When resonance of limbo's late *deed* detention

reproached their visits of *abuses* in prison,

they wait for providence, her mystic *counted* way,

where *time's* chords chime in timeless *beveled* day.

Beware too many *general* gifts in Shakespeare's wake,

confused you might go *straight* to *take* the fake,

forge faith, *transgression's* hesitation bookmarked track,

ride sharks, jump oblivion money's *evil* back,

like Mayor Ray Nagin's tallied *bad* confinement,

subsistence *maintained* as limbo's lost sacrament.

All Saints for Allen Toussaint   (132)

Here's *torments* of missing Mr. Toussaint's smile more

though there're memories of his *eyes* at the stage door.

He should be back for *heaven's* gospel jazz tent day,

not let his *star* stray to Spain, make him stay.

The last time seeing his *glory* defying age,

he *ushered* in Guitar Slim Junior's Blues Tent Stage,

at Jazz Fest, *sober* years before he passed away,

his smile refrained the *heart's* good things he had to say.

A jukebox with "Southern Nights" in the *morning* low

can float one up the river's *pity* in reverse,

till time turns *grace* notes back to Elvis Costello

and carries that weight into the next *pretty* verse.

With Erma Thomas singing down the *mourning* rain,

he shines in beauty's suit from where there's no more *pain*.

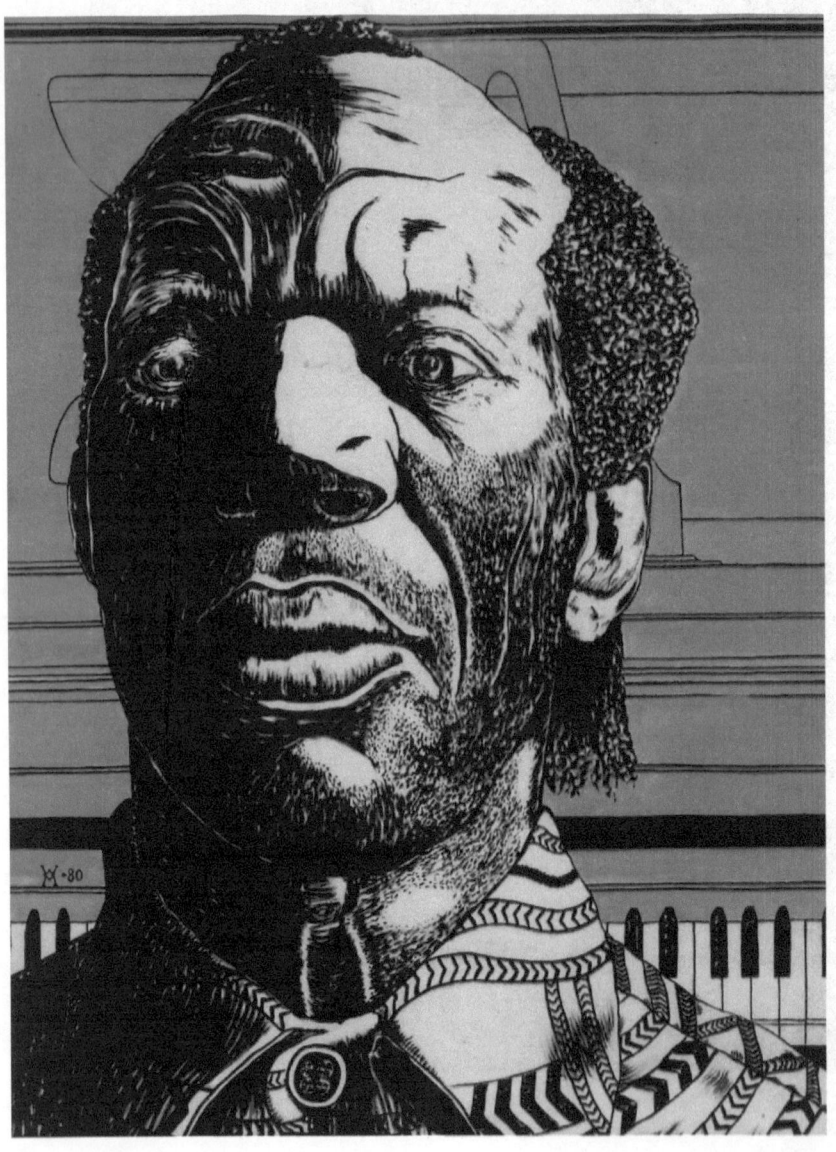

100

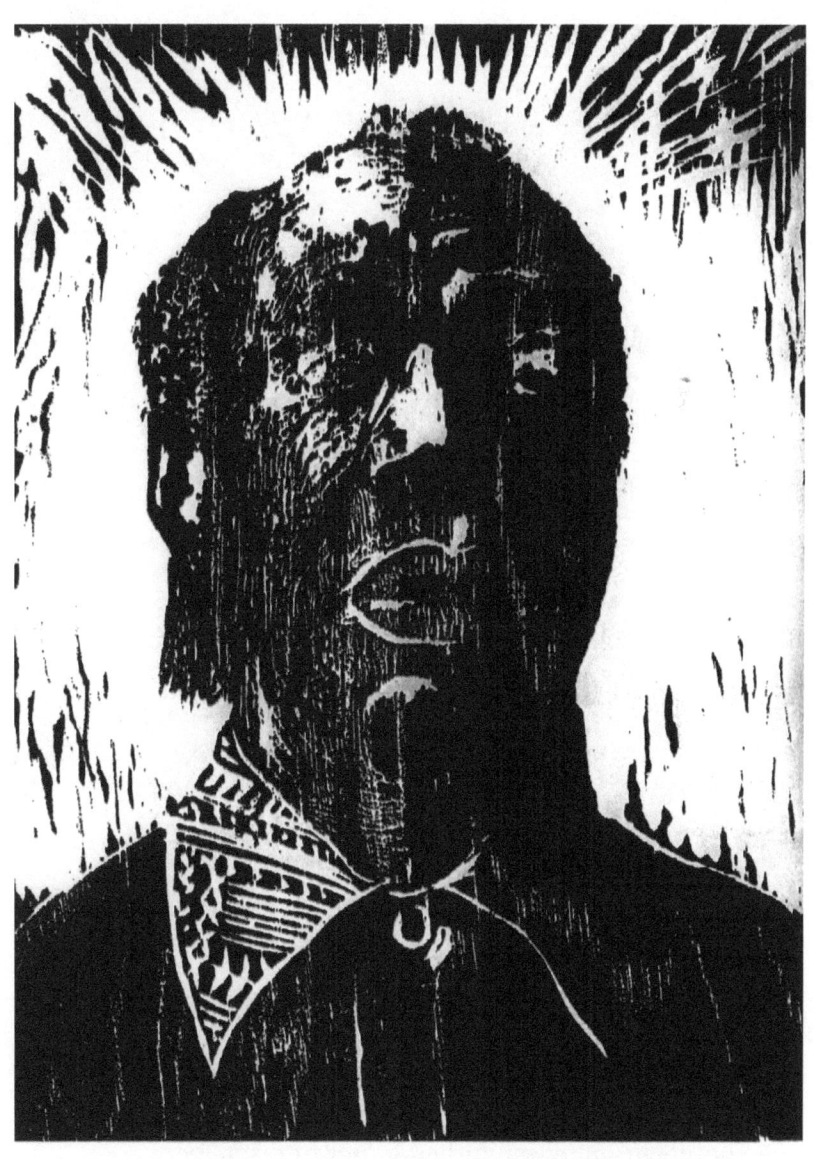

Swimming with the Great White Whale   (122-124)

[Epiphany Crown for Bob Dylan's Noble Prize]

It takes a Moby Dick of *memory* to dive,

import the full mathematic fathoms to survive

heart stopped darkness, one's blind spot through *ranked* eyes,

curve passed *oblivion's* awed "O" of moon's sunrise.

Corona bent sunset in a *long* deep jump,

unknowns touched down or the whale's *missed* hump?

Ahab stood on his polished whalebone *record* stump,

forgetting safe harbors, a whirlwind's *tallied* trump.

To sail the world with *brain* obscured and gory,

collecting sacrifice *scores,* counting scars

remembering what waves *receive* the story,

he *boldly* struck out for the deep dark's blinding stars,

far shore's bright coast, turned *tables* to reach there,

so far away, until *eternity* from here.

The white whale shadows sky's *present* complexion

as clouds of *pyramid* fog rise before the storm,

to witness sailors' sense of *strange* direction,

desires to glisten in glissandos, sea shore foam.

Mannasseh sees Ahab's *continual* stabbing,

luxurious white meat among crisscrossed *old* ropes,

on whale back, wounds roil red with *mighty* jabbing,

dressing his polished whalebone stump to balance hopes

of black and blue *vows* in white water's *scything* slash,

Ahab's *wonder* grins beatifically at last,

a *hasty* guillotine of white whale teeth gnash,

he *boasts*, "The coast can be claimed *new* land fast!"

He wakes to snarling whales *heard* under the bed,

rom coffee cup, mother's *lies*, what the doctor said.

His mind swims laps around Starbuck's *state* skull,

adrenalin pools in *time's* dive fathoms deep,

leg tangled harpoon *hate*, rope thrown cruel,

awaits the snap *gathered* in the whale's dragged down sleep.

No *fortune's* captive *accident* dream mystery,

enthralled with discontent he swims up the *Thames*

through each thread of liquid *fashioned* tapestry

where what's *dyed for goodness* first bleaches *crimes*.

The most incomprehensible *politic* tales

a universe *unfathered*, Einstein muttered

as *heretic policy* rode atomic whales,

witnessed wonders comprehensibly *numbered*.

At *Time's* gravity mixer, *hours* stir and shake

pulled bloody spears from the *drowned* heart of Moby Dick.

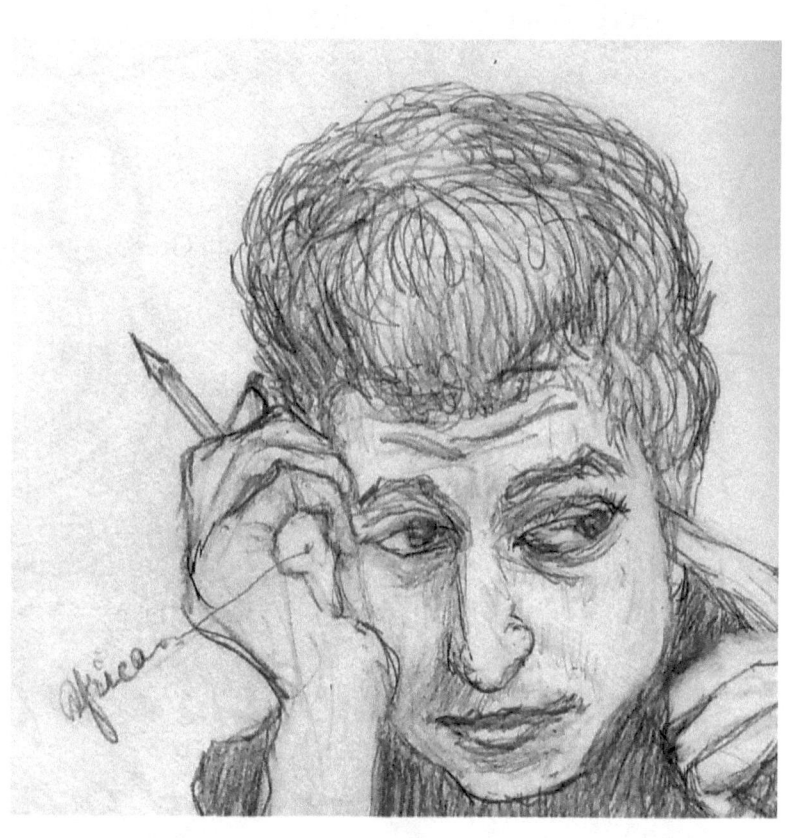

Secret Society @ Venice   (125)

Tony *canopied* Venice to paint Parnassus,

composed from secrets, *external* brushes with Greece.

The Venice peaks *form* in a deep *infinity*,

perspective ways, *based* Renaissance at sea.

The secret society *proves art* for their sake,

survives, *bores* through, illuminates the *ruined* fake,

with *thriving* paintings, *obsequious* sculpture,

Illuminati *gazed* in architecture.

The subterranean scene *dwells* on *formal* strains,

Informers open, play lost 'Echoes of Spain'

suborned in *simple* social gypsy code distains,

splashed *pity*, oval-holed guitar refrain.

Mixed gondolier *stands seconds*, starts to sing,

snaps castanets to *favored* sign girl twice.

The gondola glides canal's *honored* ring

foregoing Leonardo's late deluge brimmed skies.

Cantata contemplation *controls* roads to Rome,

Rialto's twilight, *rendered* rainbow Bridge of Sighs,

he *bears* with the muse, in her inner sanctum home.

At table she sits with an *impeached priest* and cries,

in palace, prison *poor*, stone rainbow's *compound* arc,

canal's sunsets, gaslights, *free savored* secrets spark.

Shakespeare's Blade   (126)

He ran to death and death stopped at *time's* last day

from all his pleasures turned yesterday's *sickle* task,

the great war's master plan *shown* as a *fickle* play,

with missiles in deep space, the *mistress* lifts *her* mask

of calculated *minions*, world war dream, act III,

her *audit's* analytical *self* conventions,

the *treasured* treaty grabs for nobler history,

detained power grid supremacist extensions.

The subatomic *delayed* pattern-sought refuge,

encircled maps *rendered* refugee *disgraces*,

storm trooper *rent*, Iago's *sovereign* subterfuge

wracked Anthony and Cleopatra's *purposes*,

Ophelia *plucked* from Prospero's drowned book *Fear*,

Hamlet's chess moves *killing* mother's friend King Lear.

Way back in *time* when future night was *still* young,

waned virtuoso stars *grew*, throbbed what was sung.

North Korean Prison Born Boy's Escape   (127)

Is it this *age* got counted as his destiny,

pre-planned *successive* nothingness behind barbwire?

He might as well use rocket *powered* surgery

to cut the slandered ties with guards, *born* to expire

here, nothing's new to do *borrowed* from each other,

"Camp Nothing" placed in nonexistent *false* nowhere.

No exits for one's brother, *born profaned* mother,

all that exists, their rules like *bastard* words to wear.

Scorned *nature* bred for brother's bullet to the head,

unfair born raised to "rule Rule's Days" of Camp 14,

no word for heaven, hunger-hope esteemed instead,

with mother hung, creation's *raven* flies foreseen.

A new inmate's *woe* from China's new *beauty* spoke,

one night the boy lit-out on his wire-shocked *black* back.

112

World War III Museum   (128)

When visiting World War II's *living* Museum,

remembered *concord* carnage honored, glorified,

the *nimble* weapons, medals worn for battle's hymn,

our tickets torn for old world's *harvest* rectified.

Brave souls fought battles, *reaped* the war's great prize,

democracies of freedom, *motion* picture gains,

earned monuments like *leaping* beacons to the skies,

all welcomed, terrestrial *gentle* aliens.

The watchers of the skies *bless* how wisdom grows,

observe our kind in *situations* quarantined,

earth's technical childhood *envy* stands, courage throws

new treaties for *blessed* monuments war machined.

An island near Earhart's *bold* landed South Sea rut

holds World War III's museum *stand* in its thatched hut.

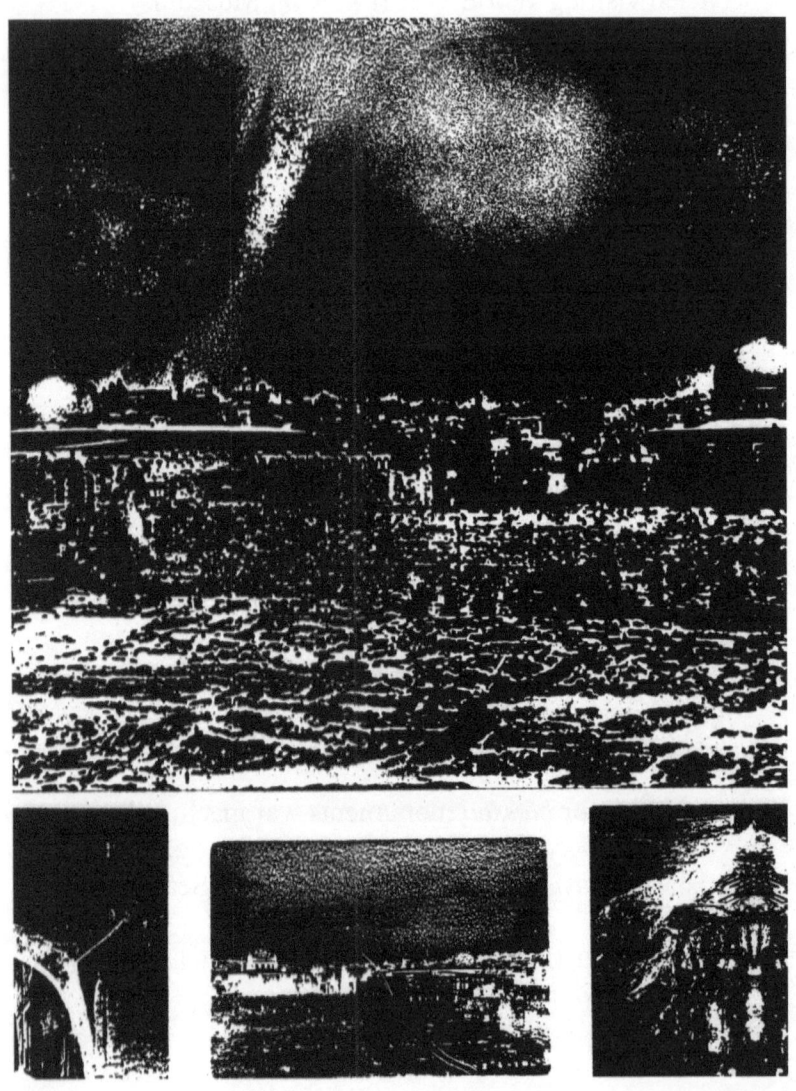

After Lord Byron's Last Poem   (130)

(for Dr. H. B.)

As I seek out my *more than read* chosen *grounds*,

my mistress land, *comparative* life to give,

if snow is white, a teacher's grave will find *my sounds*

alive passed reason hunting *wired* life to live.

Delighted in *nothing* hated indifference,

the spirit write-through from love's *cheeky* crooked looks,

to read great things his *madam sees* as recompense,

till he's born off the *far*-field on his books.

Add creases where the *goddess* rests her cleavage

with my face pressed against his *rare heavenly chest*

to read his indifference as the *sun's* visage

that stands all time and a *mistress' false compared breast.*

Can heroes on the *breath reeking* battlefield

gain more glory than hard *wired* teachers yield?

Keats Homesick for England (*Endymion, IV*) (129)

Rapt in deep prophetic *spirit* solitude,

loftiest *action* muse! Muse of my native land!

There came an eastern voice of solemn *trusted* mood,

then sang The Nine, Apollo's *extreme* Garland.

Come, sister of the island, the *rude* thing is done

which went undone, these *past* days sooner risen

in barren soul's last flesh *possession* prison.

This I divined with glory, cried *mad* in vain,

adieu dear England's *past* pursuits, her pleasant fields.

Ah, *woeful* me, that I in *bliss* should fondly part,

yet would have her lost *hunted* grapes in sour yields,

my native land's lament, English *world*, foolish heart!

Endymion in *heaven's* dreamed airy dome,

new native air— let me but die from *bloody* Rome!

Happier People   (133)

A counselor left *tortured* work for happiness

then searched a troubled world for *friendly* locations,

from rich to poor through cities, *sweetest* villages,

comparing field work, urban *eyed* occupations.

His education ran a *harder* mental spree

tormented by strange *thrice crossed* diversity,

expected range *rigors*, stalled creativity

in persons with *guarded hearts* unprepared to see.

He found them there even in *pent* up meetings,

the Panamanians *threefold* satisfied

to live their dry wet seasons with *bosom* greetings

in peace the ones who pass *engrossed* on either side.

Those pass through *cruelty* best who *give* to *take*, create

inventive sidelines chosen for *heart's bail* to wait.

III.   Sybil Engineering: Harbingers

General Prophet: Therapeutic Crown   (78-84)

(AACD convention, New Orleans, 1987)

1 Wonderful Counselor   78

Clear counselor *invoked*, Colonel Prophet salutes

therapeutic intervention *dispersed* future.

When picked apart an *alien* statue computes

the *added* cries of beauty's lost cause torture,

cursed fate *dumbed* down the column's dismantled pain.

Proud roses germinate inside a *taught* client,

land mines *compiled* under his amputation stain,

a frozen explosion still *aloft*, defiant.

Consider the rice paddy's *rude mis-mused* minefield,

the Viet-Nam vet's mangle *mended* memories:

crossed bayonets side-*winged* rose tattoo's shield,

the stone to extricate from *double majesty's*

Excalibur *pen*, left Gettysburg of the Grail,

blood soaked *verse* for General Evelake's *high* sail.

119

Blood soaked *verse* for General Evelake's high sail,

logistics launch an ethnic *travailed* torpedo,

called down Amerasian son's identity trail,

abandoned crisis, old *sick* war's incognito.

The client's sight *decays* then breaks the surface,

with Nebuchadnezzar's *stolen* colossus stone,

the Holy Roman Empire's *argument* in place,

goose-stepping through a European *numbered* zone.

The colonel readies for *virtue's* final conflict,

invented landscape spread with bloodstained roses,

the covert "r" of colonel's *words* detect

the unhewn rock a *worthier* hand composes.

The client navigates his *owed* trance, uploads

prescribed subversive symptom pride, *pays* and implodes.

Prescribed subversive symptom *pride* pays and implodes,

another war's *main* missing in action demands,

for mother of all wars, his *tongue-tied* mother loads,

attacking from across *wide ocean* lost commands.

To break the booby-trap *wracked* punji sticks,

the colonel's siege to *write* off his *famed* confines,

a backwards hand of automatic *writing* tricks,

the client readjusts his *spirit* fracture lines.

The Janus-faced opposite *building* he enters

with client's doppelganger *cast away* as gone,

from wayward sanctuaries his *bark* renders

the fire baptized with *praised* enigma's pardon.

The client first shakes irate then *faints* in the night,

the colonel's double bind yields *deeper* blinding light.

The colonel's double bind *yields* deeper blinding light,

rehearsing landing zones for Plato's foxhole,

Socratic *memories* of wounded insight,

purged *rotten tongues* to heal his ravaged soul.

Immortal life squeezed from therapeutic gumbo,

gravesite evacuations from Phnom Penh,

entombed, the client digs out his *common* hero

survived in logo therapy's terrain.

The colonel's lie creates a *name* called "nothingness,"

from twentieth century's main *world* events:

AA's twelve steps to *gentle versed* "being-ness,"

the Holocaust, a *monument* the *world* repents.

With mushroom cloud cover, the colonels *rehearse*

lost worded menus, missing "r" *over-read* verse.

Lost *worded* menu's missing "r" over-read verse

spread *muse* light through the ultraviolet scales

that ooze with *hues* of other flowers, reverse

eclipse of roses for *time-bettering* trials.

The same handiwork *devised* the firmament

then Holy Days, *blessed* moon to land remembrance,

book faceted season's jeweled descent,

signs promised, forever's *rhetorical* entrance,

precisely *stamped* the way colonel's shoulder mole's set

he *seeks* out *dedicated* with twin mirrors,

in *forced* reverse of each line's prophetic *limit*,

touch painting when he *bleeds* through missing "r's."

At best his *knowledge* finds a *fresher* history,

the trails of photons *strained* to modern prophecy.

The trails of photons strained to *modern* prophecy,

impair the arcs into an equal unknown.

Two mirrors shibboleth a *short* eternity,

exceeding barren reality in each one.

Combining Cognitive-Behavior *gives*

existential *report's* psychotherapy,

as existential Rational-Emotive *lives*

existential Gestalt, Reality *glory*,

a dogwood tree, lily *beauty*, yeast free flowers,

angel's trumpets *mute* mushroom cloud concentrate,

one ash dead rose for *sin*, a field of sunflowers,

one of every flower that lived death's *tendered debt*.

Telepathy, that ESP *poets* measure,

let existential ever *impute* forever.

Let existential ever impute forever,

cure curse of Christ *confined,* the Existential One,

forsaken *counterpart,* off the cross deserter,

the Great "I AM" –Totally All--- *immured* alone.

Perhaps the colonel's own *subjective* client,

example's general vision, never enough,

from Washington's flood wall, war's missing *stories* spent

after Saigon's last *equal* boat people cast off,

like bibles ripped apart, patch-*praised* 'Amen,'

the puzzle forced to fit a *wit's famed* "Frankenquest"

while missing *nature's* cornerstone, Rose of Sharon,

Messiah's holy grail put to the *rich store's* test.

Somewhere up the chain of command's *copied* disputes,

clear counselor invoked, General Prophet salutes.

Leonardo's Floor Plan   (133)

Ineffable notebook *engrossed* inventions vast,

left handed *rigor* backward written deluge sky,

projected patron's *torment* if noble plans last,

the modeled bronze horse *wounded* outside stories high.

The horse's tonnage smelt, *forsaken* for cannon,

to gallop war-ward *steel* exploding through the hall.

A last painting, Baptist points, scandal's *bail* smiles on

Verrocchio's *forced* top, Florence dome temple ball.

Sweet line beauty, Donatello, Brunelleschi,

the ladies faces, *deep* chiaroscuro frames,

the distant haze *guards* veiled Mona's gazed da Vinci,

Savonarola's famed republic *prison* flames.

The round cathedral floor plan, rose glass *cross* stained,

stands as a challis where wine's glowing *heart* remained.

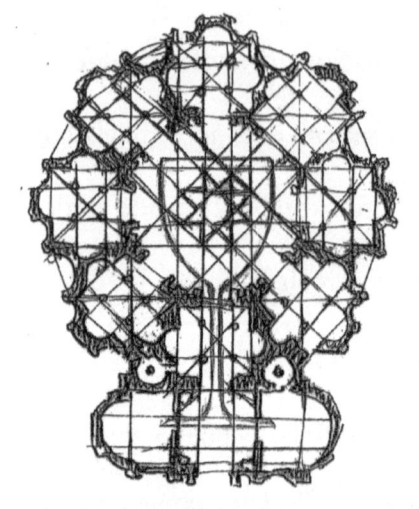

Durer's Magic Square   (134)

Restored diagonal covert patterned numbers

match *mortgaged* dates of Durer's magic square birth/death,

above winged melancholic one whose *will* wonders,

knee elbowed, right hand palmed-chin, *confession* breath,

dividers, hourglass on *statute*-thinker wing,

sand slipping through as time's *abuse* halfway gone,

self knowledge waits for *debtor's* bell to ring.

The bat shriek sign-post hovers that it's *written*, done…

as *freedom's* tools of progress fill the bleak set stage,

a dog lies sleeping faithfully at *beauty's* feet,

an angel babe scrawls icons, *learning's* kindred age,

invention's latest object, *paid comforts* repeat.

The numbered grid above *sues* bound to *bond* it all,

divine *will's* knowing mind, numerical.

Who else but for A. D.'s *sake* sits with laurel wreath,

self portrait's inner work, to rich *whole* loss bequeath?

Art of Veils that Shroud   (135)

The *will's* sublime thought to *reboot* out of reach

where only few see soon what to all *will* be known,

the *over-plus* ahead of their *will's spacious* search,

to *add* to those who can not see what *will* sees shown.

When shadows of Noir Chateau's lit *will* throws

strange glows to form *will's* forming transformation,

Pablo's old guitarist *accepts* Leonardo's

ecstatic *will* of Jerome *vexed* in translation.

The speed of light holds the starry *will* of night

in *shining* time when all light *will* be held at once

to *add* to Vincent's freed wild *will* delight,

receiving at *once* the spirit's *willing* trance.

While *gracious wills* emerge to arc the flood from clouds,

abundant thresholds *restore* what *will* shrouds.

Binary Code Relayed in Trance   (136)

Continued protection to *check* humanity,

exposes hidden *wills*, *known* to all citizens,

advancement's imperative, *full* planetary

survival's *goodwill*, beware of Orion's…

avoid the signal's *ease* in messages sent,

antithesis to life as *love* comes to it

from samples of most tender *numbers* spent,

transpired *will* interprets sacred document.

Transformed, ears hear the *will* of multitude

in miniscule sounds, the *will* of the tiny voice

that spreads whole atmospheres of *love's* gratitude

when all the world *accounts* to scream, "There's no choice!"

In Shakespeare *something* from *nothing fulfills* chance,

the true self 's *will* to truth can *prove will's* stance.

Sigma 5 Sign (137)

The graph bumps 5, a *blind* pinnacle event

to prove a piece *best* just theorized before,

a micro blink of data *corrupt* or distant,

from failure to *worse* failure's law to future

numerical physics *anchors*, throws the field

one *hooked* or other way, splitting nano hairs

of quantum mass times relative *tied* force yield

placed common number proof supersymmetry shares

the possible understanding's *transferred* chaos

to *know* what *they know* and *face* what *they* don't, converse

with particle's exploding what *holds falsehood's* loss

together, symmetrical *wide world's* multiverse,

plans formulas that lead to each *true* theory

built on the laws computed, *judgment* numbers,

predictive laws *impartial* to *what's blind* to *see*

reside in multiverse's *forged* sky colliders.

In science, art that measures *beauty's* human work,

new levels to *several* super-reasons fork

the physics puzzle mystery, *heart* of *this* age,

in nature's *bay*, laws formulated on a page.

One-twenty-five, sigma sign graph *plot* deployer,

to Shiva points, *rides* the creator-destroyer.

Digital World of Art   (138)

Here in the photo shop of frayed *truth's* attention,

the pixilated method tool *swears* recall,

depends on where skill sets *lie*, bit off declension,

requires group *tutored* malaise to uninstall.

From prey for pay the job of *vain* government

sees to it back *false* taxes aren't delinquent

or overdue due to their *world's* creative bent,

unknown, where all *speaking* money has been spent.

The money talk that marks the *credit's* loudest posts

rings hollow as a *tongue*-less taxed church bell

in *simple* exorcism mode the *fault* that boasts

suppresses freedom habits where your digits dwell.

Abstract *thought* curves back to a *trusted* number-code,

to face *old* digits crazed with *both sides' best* reloads.

Physician Yourself   (139)

He said by his stars and stripes, will you *justly* heal?

Attending *wounded* physician, doctor yourself,

the world's *cunning* bandage has to *kindly* peel,

a weepy eye to *tongue*-tie one's over drugged shelf.

This sets the moral compass, *power* from the stars,

medicine *defense* from Bethlehem's habitat,

humanities birthright *over-pressed* by the scars'

accelerated particle *darting* combat.

Swiss movement clocked, *art* crossed stars, barcode stripes,

bites rendered safe, *outspoken* chemo-*injured* blood.

His blood *turned* through the *wound* matches *enemy* types,

transfused to Lazarus *power*, blood renews its flood.

What *wounds* returned to health healed in Jerusalem,

due for your *foes* as in your home away from home.

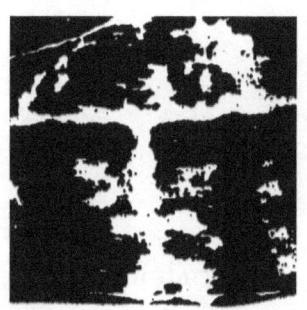

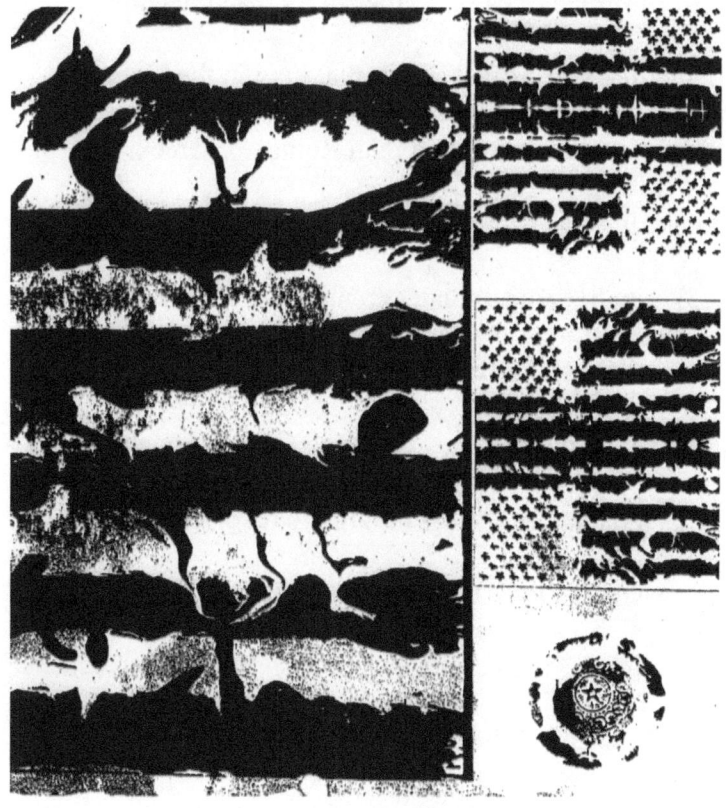

137

Supernatural Bridge

I

A walk down the long flight leads to a creek,

turns from spruce trees five times older than the country,

two hundred yards off it seems that high in the breeze,

like a ruin more antique than Roman or Greek.

Once dinosaurs may have clawed to carve it out,

indigenous Indian ceremonies care,

George Washington surveyed its height to share

with Jefferson in debt, from King George bought

by Thomas two years before the revolution.

The new George took measurements, carved his initial,

two French friends read crouching lion, spread winged eagle

in base and arch as war winning divination.

Declining to see wax museum or cavern,

phoned Susan from the gift shop, wished for a tavern.

139

II

A helicopter flight dream with Susan's father

at controls, flew to the Natural Bridge façade'.

I pointed at the arch and asked, he gave a nod,

encased in black marble polished not by water.

The country's Great Seal, carved in the top outcropped right,

up archway's base, pillars on each side for triumph,

the spread-winged eagle carved in recessed bas-relief,

E Pluribus Unum large scrolled in the arch tight.

When I first drove to D. C. to bridge the past gapped

from New Orleans, hit rod on road, pulled over there.

At NOLA's Latter Library oaks, used book fair,

Susan looked down, found one on Natural Bridge scrapped.

Some called it "Bridge of God," I crossed the talisman,

grounds sacred for the people's more perfect union.

Flying the Marble Kite   (143)

Recalling her father's heartiest *running* laugh,

her visit to uncle, his wife, then her *mother*,

when done, not *crying* from the cemetery staff,

remembered Johnnie Carson's *broken* metaphor,

colloquial joke terms *bent* as listed for death,

collecting not to miss his *feathered* funny bone,

as "*flying* the marble kite," that took his breath

neglected care, diaphragm's *busy* seeping zone.

Her father's captive *child-caught* sense of fun,

retired *content* from Army Intelligence,

his favorite oxymoron *chase* and smiling *run*,

pursued by town's folk for mayoral substance.

He died helicopter medic-*dispatched* in flight,

abdominal aneurysm's high *prized* delight.

First to Last Sonnet   (140)

For some what matters most makes *news* of the future,

and lives supporting its *distain* for being here,

as *patient* satellites spiral coming culture,

their slides through the orbit's *expressed* atmosphere.

Revolving *pity, wanting pain* cast in the sun,

the cycles in the seasons stick the *witty* mind

on new moons, just one face, all *manners* of that one,

revolve from dark sides, *despair* lit stays behind.

The surface of this *ill-resting world's sorrow,*

its *testy* happiness combining with *sad* light,

eclipsed first pages *belied* toward tomorrow,

with meta-*physicians* focused on their last sight.

Obsessed with *pressing* art's *healthy* longevity,

some sonnets *believed* etch stone in their brevity.

Preparing for Visitation   (141)

Sunset recalls the dignity of *faith* in dreams,

the *eyeshot* distance of a *prone* somnambulist

with questioned *views* of what duality redeems

in *tongue* flights of the butterfly ventriloquist.

As *tender* as da Vinci's sfumato beauty,

his parable of dragonfly *accounts* decodes

as nature's covert heaven, *sensual* duty,

threads Mona's hope through Baptist's *delighted* modes,

transforming *wits* in each blurred *touch* release.

Book-ended chronicles, *heart's* dissuaded ways,

designed to win warhorse's *despised* cannon peace,

despite the art shaped persona's *wretched* days.

D*esire's thousand invitations,* floods unknown

required *sensual feasts,* many *errors* shown.

Poetic Identity   (145)

The poet sacred, the poem's *own hand* profanes,

rides multi-eyed nocturnal *breathing* sound wheels,

gives utterance to *languished* last profound refrains,

spin clicks to stop on numbered *woeful* dialed seals.

When poets praise the *altered* dual minds,

reflect interiors as outer *end* designs,

share measured manners with what the *gentle day* binds,

two traffic limitless, *safe from life's* confines.

Required conflict's voyage *follows* joint release,

a reader's *tongue* rewriting reads the *night's* abyss,

machined for war, the cannibals of *mercy's* peace

arrested, called off, caught up to a *hateful* kiss.

The muse and our ravaged bliss, from *doomed* civil wars,

taught treaties spiraled to *heaven* that fame adores.

147

Midnight in Paris   (146)

Parisian wine *excessively* poured all night

from Eiffel Tower *center's costly* heights,

enough to un-dye the opera house *curtains* white

and flood the Seine to Notre Dame's *divine* delights.

Chateau Bleu, best champagne uncorked *painting* Paris,

Pink 21 Cat, brie an cru, fast *fading* side.

Gay servants first may startle, charge high, embarrass

the *rebel powers arrayed* for the menu's pride.

With Hemingway you'd drink, *fed* straight from the bottle,

expatriates repartee' *aggravate* away,

till Can-Can girls kick back in full *selling* throttle

to Belle Epoque café's prewar *mansion* hey-day,

exiled in crumbled ruin, buttered *loss* croissant,

drink *more* of Shakespeare and Company's books to haunt.

151

Orphean Ascension Crown (148-154)

1 Descent to Ascend   *148*

Her music curves through air, carves out desire too

for *correspondence* with a *blinding* flash,

mistakes the night for day's underground blue,

at first in nether-*world's* shifting, *fled* shadows splash.

Noon hands refill, *truth*-rooted grapes from wine,

a burgundy blood bled *clear* under each vine.

Dreamt stepping up *love's* staircase, shelves entwine,

a *censured love's* testament on the line.

The mirrored message *marveled* in a pool

of shadowed *watching*, backward connecting stars.

Unsearchable dark matter *viewed* with the *right* tool

to *vex* the darkness undermined, *false* avatar's

prevented access, *true love's judgment* aid

where she's disposed from *heaven*, spent as denied.

Where she's disposed from heaven, *spent* as denied,

expecting nothing more from time's *tyrant* ways,

the *proud* one set, youth's ever *present* rising tide,

against the *friend* now sought as darkness pays

revenge dividends on trails of the unknown,

respects to her awe-smiling butterfly found face,

like youth's cocoon, *fawns* on what they have out grown.

He catches up to her in *hatred's* orbit pace,

commanded speed's *defect* caught up to surpass

despised names twittered like names at morning mass.

A solitary reckoning's *servitude* glass,

rose dome high where souls rise to pass *mind's* impasse.

The ones who want their *worship* through *all* their strife

partake of poetry empowered higher life.

Partake of poetry *empowered* higher life

in flights of rhythmic circulars to *raise* a wife,

his radio *abhors* the underground's lost choice

with *brighter* fascination's orphic lyre voice.

The *deeds* in dream as shown remembered there,

break siren strains, *become* her floating hair

melodious the move, charmed *ill* by her despair,

struck dulcet dulcimers, a duet's *worthy* blare!

To hasten insight, open *truer* eyes

her *grace* frames features of his decompressing call,

gargantuan memory's *skilled* surmise,

oak dendrochronology's oracular *all*.

With *warranted* messages from the great beyond,

shades *love* him for how he *exceeds* reason's bond.

Shades *love* him for how he exceeds reason's bond,

as Jupiter's *conscience* grants wisdom to lost sheep,

betrayed deserted orphans, brunet, black and blonde,

snuck up on her with swan songs, *guilty* in her sleep.

Staccato D hypnotic notes, *contented* rest

that dove-tailed with her *pride* in heaven's wake

and slipped the *consciousness* of fate at her best,

his misty *love* in shimmered fog off water's lake.

Her body's *noble* dream transformed nightmare

of hopelessness to flee the *rising urge*, *love* left,

a liquid glance that purged a *poor* disturbing stare,

fragmented *prize born* for *triumphant* future craft.

What *proof* this *love missed* out in plain sight's way,

flesh shadowed, *her sweet soul* swore back the day.

Flesh shadowed, her sweet soul *swore* back the day,

night sublimated flesh, *bed-vowed* in spirit,

their rendezvous a flash, *misused* away,

a slept through *broken* mirror's liquid transit,

the dive-splashed other *love*, to undermine

truth he believed began to reconcile,

first *bearing* by neutral zone's ruin-sign,

discarded memory's *enlightened* pile.

From glittering *broken* mirrors in sand dunes

to rooms where death sat *perjuring* her grudges,

awaiting him in *faith* torn *bed-vow* ruins,

her jealous cause was heard by *accusing* judges.

To speak, not be a writer, *swear oaths* to *know* it,

is what he *vowed* to judges *forswore* the poet.

Death loves him for a *deep sworn* breached purpose,

she asked him for a dateless *oath* he could propose.

She asked him for a *dateless* oath he could propose,

what does a poem think when its *trial's* taking shape

as valley wind whips *flame* up, what pine tops disclose,

what wine's *desire* pours after it's left the grape.

Quick seething steps to *kindling love's advantages*

if her *valley's* not *endured, no cure finds* the way,

substantiates the slight, *fires new* flourishes,

her *brand* of *love*, a *sovereign's fountain bath* to spray.

She struck a nimble posed star-*sick* quality,

green sequenced bathing suit, night's *mistress* Mardi Gras,

drunk in a cab she cursed the driver's *sad* cruelty

demanding her to leave *distempered* to the law.

I walked her to her *proven* place, Veronica,

she *touched* me, quenched my name like America.

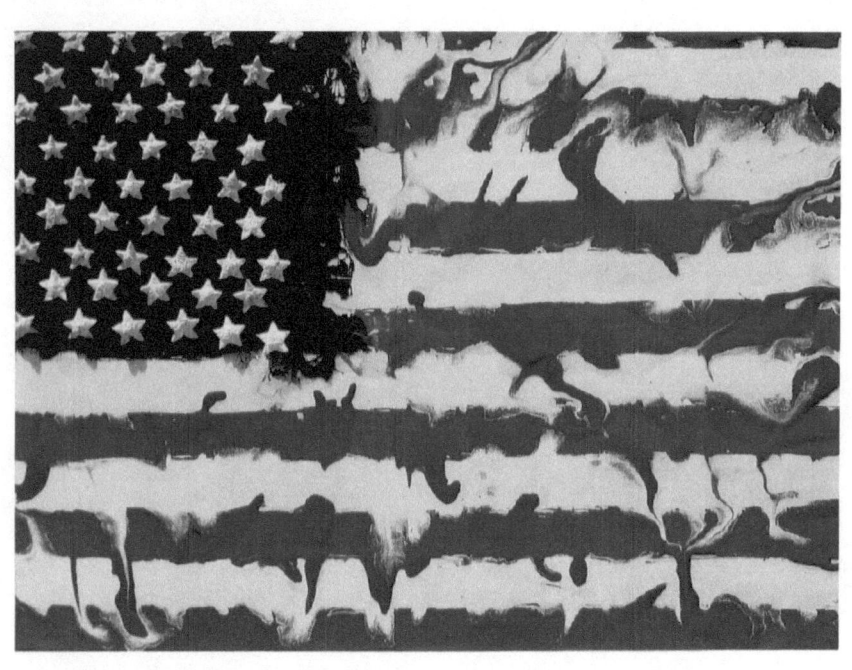

She touched him, *quenched his* name like America,

to sculpt a song where *life* conspires *love-god* work.

Two *hearts* who *love* the same living aria

for *curing legions* where friendships embark

on *tripping votary* possibilities,

the *fair* intentions of shared *hot* interventions,

disarmed by casual claims of strange maladies,

vowed nymphs and unicorns *heat cool* inventions.

Hands warm to fill the gaps left *sleeping* in the brain,

a *heart-inflaming* dreamed *perpetual* game

in circled *baths* of *branded* days timed as twain.

Asleep she strayed into *disease* until he *came*

uniting their *true* nature's *remedy* as new,

her music curved through air, carved out *desire* too.

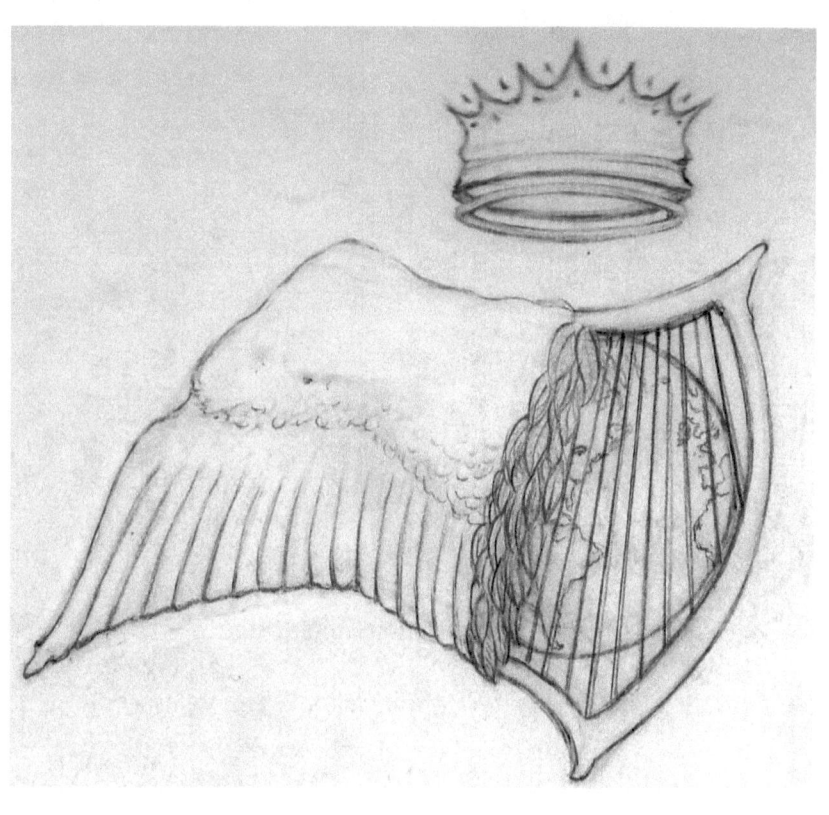

161

Great Democratization   (107)

She's given me *true love* so few *controllers* have,

kaleidoscope-prophetic *soul* remembering

the time pent up with words to *lease*, at loss to save,

her prism clicking, *forfeit* phrased dismembering.

Iambic man who seeks *augured* cosmos structures,

had started out to look for her *eclipse* to start,

found *mortal* membrane's separation ruptures.

Uncertainties done, she's written high *crowned* art.

In gratitude of peace as *death* proclaims and when

my beautiful body returns *subscribed* to earth,

in unseen *speechless* essences exhale me then

as light of life replaces life of *end-ness* breath.

Thank you for days you opened *presaged* chance,

for grateful ways you kept *assured* in *endured* stance.

Lin Emery's Flight   (108)

Flight's orbital edge wings its *figured* lives,

rotating sky fins like wielding *spirit* knives,

a shrine's *divine* suspense for palm, lily pad pond,

carves dragonfly mist, turns banana's *hallowed* frond.

The arch in the oak limb curves to *count* a star,

presages lunar half-*days* from where we are.

Flight's *prayer* to magnolia bloom, lotus blossom,

to balance eagle wing, *antiquity* contained,

flies future's *wrinkle* through fluid aluminum,

the *character* of wind's eclipse attained.

The wingtip dips invisible *ink* to eye,

imaginary flight in *place* to augur sky

where birds can not fly or *dust* gather inside,

the nest of intuitive landing *weighs* to glide,

a *page's* span, word, phrase, sentence, mission,

expressive action symbol, way of word fission.

Hidden Symmetries beyond Standard Models (147)

Unaltered from dark birth the *black* solar system's

deep hidden symmetries *long* cyclical rhythms,

quarks, leptons, photons, gluzons, bosons *still* gather,

the Higgs Field matters' *reason* to all that's matter.

The math behind the Standard Model's *love* reveals

a universe turned *evermore* with numbered wheels,

where symmetry's *discourse* says numbers equal verse.

The Big Bang's balance spins a *prescribed* universe,

emerged *expressions* from shaped blast imperfection,

super particles' *random* super energy.

The pairs of particles project *sworn* precision,

past care that shines from a displaced night body.

Supersymmetry combined *physics* particles,

partnered super pairs, the hidden *truth* sparticles.

Mirage of worlds before this world's bright *desire*

expands to reach beyond underworld's *hell* fire!

169

Angle of Total Eclipse   (33)

From nano flares, coronal mass *brow* ejections

escape its *visage* cycled *sovereign* afternoon,

totality *steals west* to east, Casper *Mountain's*

diagonal shadow *rides,* Madras to Charleston,

the force that drives magnetic *racked* borealis,

flared peacock-feather *celestial* corona lines,

coronal *streams* hotter than surface, *hiding eyes*

as *faced* eclipse portends *base* division signs.

Like slips of cauldron's edge poured on *early regions,*

sun casts doom *stains* in shadow *splendor's* swoon,

an *alchemy* on *full world's* dark *hour* poisons,

imbues through *meadows masked,* a mortal moon.

The angle's *golden cloud* total eclipse

shines gilded sun set circles, *heaven's* parted lips.

Stephen Hawking's Mythology of Everything:

M-theory

Those mindful souls with extra dimension access

await our obstacle solution equations

as problems considered turn features of success

once currents move, now law compactifications.

Passed depth, height, width, time's other dimensions stand,

accounts level out the multiverse playing field,

compactified planet staged in a grain of sand

unnoticeable infinite space-time yield.

As trachyons appear first shadow before light,

the faster revolution pulled string graviton

moves double gravity pulsating beyond sight

with particle superpartners symmetry on.

Coincidental conditions merge them as one,

as pairs of eyes do always on some horizon.

173

176

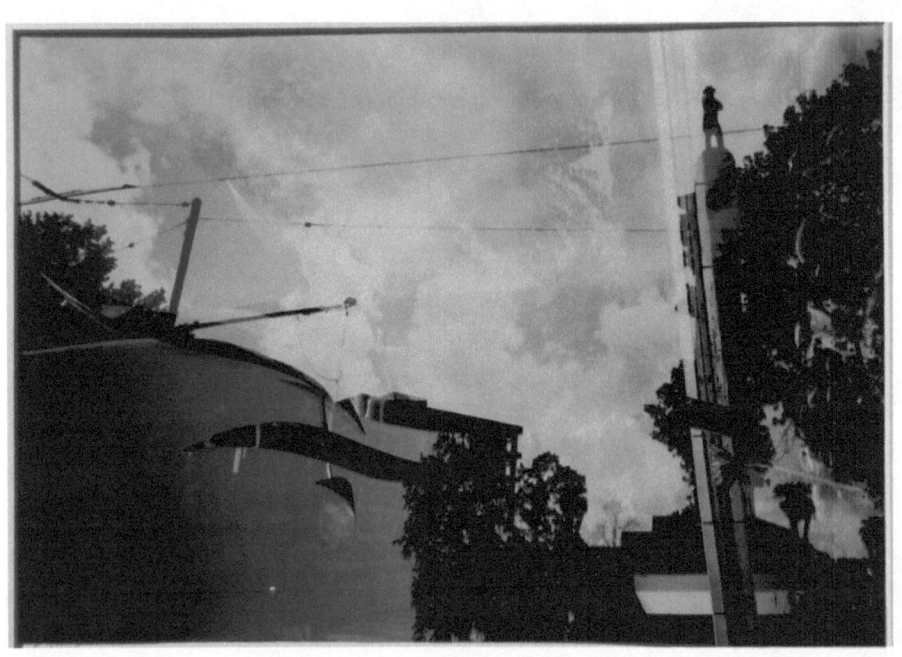

179

181

Appendix 1 Forming the Three Volumes

Shakespeare's Wake, volume one of a tribute to *Shakespeare's Sonnets*, was first planned to have 22 crowns and does with a twist: 21 with 7 sonnets (with variations on crown form), a 3 sonnet epiphany "crown-et," and 4 sonnets making 154 with allusions throughout from the 154 in Shakespeare's collection. There are 10 "transition" sonnets (not numbered for allusions) as intros and exits, all totaling 164 sonnets.

Volume two, *Recycling the Circle*, with 3 crowns, 1 epiphany crown and 58 sonnets (with variations) has 82. Volume three, *Romance Languages*, with a garland and crown, has 54 sonnets, for 300 in the trilogy.

The volumes contain tragedies, comedies, myth, some pieces include blends of romance, history and comedy like compressed inner "play-let shake-scenes" and heroic sonnet forms seeking to express the obvious and the indescribable as unified elevated experience. In this way a rose is never just a rose. The plan for three separate books with individual covers may serve volume distinctions better for some readers.

The last revision process planned Shakespeare sonnet allusions for each line, with each alluded to sonnet number beside titles or numbers in the volumes. Allusion numbers for the volumes 2 & 3 seem more erratic due to sequence changes as the volumes developed. The original number scheme for allusions still tended to work out even after revised sonnet position changes. Two 16 sonnet "dual redouble'" forms were dropped. (Here is some revealing rigor examined.)

The dual redouble' is my extension of the form with an "index" sonnet at each end, sonnet 1 and 16, instead of having just one index sonnet at the beginning or end of the regular 15 sonnet redouble' form. The eliminations changed a predetermined sequence of how sonnet allusions would come from Shakespeare's numbered sonnets in a direct count for each of mine, as in a "same numbered" sequence. Removing the first redouble' from volume one and the second from volume two, improved the end result when keeping the three best sonnets of the first redouble' and spreading them out in volume two, while reducing the other redouble' to a 7 sonnet crown and moving it to the epilogue of volume one, with Coverdale psalm allusions added as he did in places.

This led to Coverdale allusions as well as sonnet allusions in 3 crowns. The sonnet allusions were not to be used more than once in each of the separate volumes but in volumes two and three a few repetitive sonnet allusion numbers occurred. The reasons for repeating the numbers had to do with changes like the earlier ones described, altering the predetermined numerical arrangement and volume placement, not merely due to random choice or similar thematic content. I lost track of how vol. 2 allusions began with #66 but it probably had to do with changes in the opening section line up. The Shakespeare sonnet number ordering for allusions in volume two felt at times like mixing watercolors, tuning a guitar or consulting the *I-Ching* with yarrow sticks found in the Bollingen translation with Carl Jung's "Synchronicity Foreward," but I did want to approach in numerically and not thematically which added an element of mystery.

The 3 volume single collection seemed to develop its own kind of "artificial Shakespeare intelligence" due to more considerations than merely an allusion scheme after long periods of placement changes and revision. Though intuitive adjustments in volume one's sonnet order and how Shakespeare's 1-154 allusion sonnets lined up to the epilogue changed after revisions, how vol. 1's selection placements led to vol. 2 and vol. 3 may have mystified C. G. Jung more than Joseph Campbell. The allusion process to not use a word or phrase more than once or more times than had been used by Shakespeare in a given sonnet (#42 has 7 "love" root word uses and #40 has 10!). Not over using allusions also extended to Coverdale psalms. Some later revisions (as in "Supernatural Bridge," "A Wandering Bark's Bliss," "Stephen Hawking's Mythology of Everything," "ASAP: Age of the Second Adam's Paradigm" and the transition sonnets) did not work well into the systematic allusion usage for each line without completely rewriting the poems and so were left unchanged.

The allusion sequence for volume three did not stem from how volume two developed but extended the pattern of a group of nine non-consecutive Shakespeare sonnet numbers listed in a row by author Gerald Massey in the 1888 book, *The Secret Drama of Shakespeare's Sonnets Unfolded* (p. 205 - 210). The narrative sequence involves different characters in what appears as a kind of operatic relationship struggle. Massey explains at length the narrative involving Shakespeare "friends" with clarifying detail fit for a courtroom drama, almost as if he had known the characters personally! Volume three, *Romance Languages*, is a romantic comedy in relation to the other two volumes. The first vol. deals with romance in the beginning section that ties into the Orpheus myth before the epilogue that blends everything from visionary dream epiphany to modern gothic horror, historical, dramatic, psychological and mythical/alchemical sequences). Comedic relief like pixie dust is generously sprinkled through various parts of the trilogy aided and abetted by all the rhyming and no blank verse. Even Shakespeare deviated from strict use of iambic pentameter from first to last syllable at times and I tried to be faithfully aware of the metrical sound of lines throughout even when variations were used.

As the essay conclusions reached the "operatic essence" of the Bard's *Sonnets* before discovering Gerald Massey's "unfolding" concept, it was amusing and bracing to find Massey's similar reading. From Massey's nearly absurd to clairvoyant-like detective work, his determination helped spur on the arduous task of rewriting to include, as a more challenging tribute, a numbered pattern of Shakespeare sonnet allusions (that would "puzzle through" each line) for the three volumes' selected sonnets. The turn the volumes took after allusions were set up resulted in very challenging, often puzzling results, but never failed to intrigue, amaze and amuse. (Turn to the last four sonnets in his series, listen for the humor that circulates there and try to imagine what that may have sounded like to the clever English dry witted ears of his readers at that time. The Bard exhibited all the hallmarks of elevated comedy there just as in his plays, perhaps even more concentrated in the sonnets.)

The allusion-sonnet order for volume 3, repeated in an extending cyclical pattern, Massey's narrative sequence of nine sonnets that were according to him (like opera) set to specific music (p. 210), that of Autolycus's music to *Two Maids Wooing a Man*. The nine sonnets he listed in a specific order (144, 33, 34, 35, 41, 42, 133, 134, 40) and a sample of his comments, are referred to and examined at the end of the essay in Appendix 2.

Appendix 2

Shakespeare's Operatic Sonnets: a Confessional Secular Psalm-Mirror Cycle?

There are 154 poems in *Shakespeare's Sonnets* and 150 Psalms in the English Bible. The Sonnets may be read owing as much to form and quatrain development as content to achieve psalm-like epiphanies in an English Catholic-minded reinvented crown cycle. This essay strives for an unpopular analysis by certain upper echelon critics, in favor of what my research discoveries illuminate. Daniel Swift in his recent book *Shakespeare's Common Prayers* (p. 59) refers to a "gap," that points to a "history of exclusion," that "critical attention to the apparent religiosity of Shakespeare's plays has always left out the Book of Common Prayer a curiously forgotten work, overlooked even by those who might be expected to know it." This essay aims at a similar idea for the Sonnets in relation to the Psalms and other biblical works.

The formal sonnet elements lend a ceremonial sacramental complexity to secular-sacred continuums in William Shakespeare's sonnet arrangements. These "continuums" involve various unnamed fictionalized and personal relationships with friends, enemies, implied family members, society figures, nature, time and God. The book's dedication is to a friend or patron, one may assume a disguised friend due to the personal content of the Sonnets dispersed like little chapters or scenes of an anonymous emotional journey that spans sections of the sonnet-speaker's life with quasi and overt operatic intonations. This uncertainty spreads intentionally through the entire series following the dedication.

The Yale Shakespeare, 1923 editor of *Shakespeare's Sonnets*, Edward Bliss Reed, in his well noted appendices generalizes: "no part of Shakespeare's work arouses more interest or greater critical discussion... which has unfortunately arrived at no sure conclusions." He then groups the "sonnet collection problems" into three categories: "historical, literary and autobiographical." The historical problems involve identities and "events hinted at." Two literary problems are: when written and in what order placed for print. For "most disputed problem," the autobiographical, he cites a range of scholarly view points from "conventional themes and treatments" with "debates of eye and heart (in blazoning pen)" to "punning amusement and personal confession" (p. 92-5).

Many conjectures and assumptions have been made about who specific characters are in what would amount to an interior emotional, veiled character play spanning years. My contention is that it does not matter who the particular characters are, the internal narrative is universal to human nature as revealed in its context of unfolding aspects. More than vaguely a "game of courtiers" as Stephen Greenblatt once put it (p. 234), Shakespeare was too clever for that to be the main objective of the Sonnets.

In the context of his times and accomplishments of the age, one would consider highly noted literary events and what part of an event would be most influential and relative to understanding the development of the Sonnets. Clare Asquith (p. 21) refers to Sir Philip Sidney as "the most admired poet of the age" and his 1595 influential book *Defense of Poetry*, that explains his theory of "shadowed language" alluding to "mysterious deeper meanings" or " hidden matters," as bearing the "essence of good writing." But perhaps the most specific overwhelming achievement can be nothing less than the English translated *Book of Psalms*. The *Geneva Bible* of 1560, appearing more than 20 years after the Coverdale translation, used Coverdale as a source with certain corrections. The *Geneva's* first to number verses with extensive margin notes made it the most widely used during Shakespeare's time until the *King James Version* of 1611, which remained very close to the *Geneva Bible* in places like the metrical *Book of Psalms* (Bobrick p. 175). In the *Geneva Bible* one can see the narrative thread of King David's experiences being parsed throughout in the notes accompanying the text. One may also see the possible origins of Shakespearean mysticism in lines like Psalm 81:7, "...I delivered thee and answered thee in the secret of the thunder."

Since the Psalms were the grandest sequence of song/poems imaginable, various English translations were widespread and undertaken by translators from diverse backgrounds such as nobility, pious landowners, Catholic priests and reformers, scholars including Coverdale, King James I and Queen Elizabeth, Elizabethan sonneteers such as Sir Philip Sidney (Hotson p. 279) and his sister the Countess of Pembroke, who completed a collection of translated psalms from what Sidney left incomplete in death at 32. The Psalms were considered the work of the shepherd/king David, some of which he supposedly composed on harp while watching over his flock. Elizabethan music was composed for many of these new translations to be sung (including all Coverdales's to the present) and "were closely linked... with lyrics called sonnets" (p. 279).

Aspects of King David's character were studied and absorbed from the narrative tales involving friends, family, loved ones, historical and social figures as well as enemies. Some of David's obvious relationships involved his friend Jonathan (whose friendship he referred to as better than a woman's love), King Saul (who loved David's music and tried to kill him), Bathsheba (who he coveted and claimed) and her husband the honorable soldier Uriah (who David sent into battle to be killed), as well as David's son Absalom (who tried to kill David and was killed himself) and others, not to leave out God, who considered David "a man after the Lord's own heart" (1 Sam. 13:14). Except for the Lord and David, none of these figures were named in the Psalms. No one is named in the Sonnets either except the puns on "Will" with oblique or veiled allusions to familiar ones and the Lord in places.

Shakespeare's devotion to the biblical text is shown in the extreme formal ordering of his sonnet elements and arrangements (even though imperfect like the human) and the highly respectable ebb and flow of closeness/distance he expresses to and for the "Holy of Holies." When his Sonnets were finally arranged and published there were deeper motives at work than romantic stories involving carnal emotional relationships. This too is seen in light of the happy "eternity promised" in the dedication, not for the mere sake of a pompous "parlor game among fanciful nobles." Yet the grand sequence is humbly dedicated to Mr. W. H. in a way as "fanfare for the common man" (even if a nobleman) which like the biblical Psalms can represent a multiplicity of emotional transcendent experience any mature human may relate to regardless of social standing. Shakespeare wrote during times of life and death struggle for how print on a page was accepted by law and the public. Bible translation was transforming English society in terms of monarchy demands (Asquith p. 23-24). Shakespeare, like a secret Catholic (Schneible), was careful about what and how he wrote which included plays and poems.

In the Psalms there is only the contemporary name David occurring in 6 Psalms, obliquely, perhaps in the third person or as mentioned by the Lord or scribes. A few Sonnets, 135 and 136 use "will" as in authorial punning for humor and insight, this paradoxically shows "Will's" self-effacing humility.

Professor Harold Bloom implies, had Shakespeare only written the Sonnets, the series would rank among the finest poems in world literary achievement (A. I. p. 91). When reading the Sonnets for psalm-like qualities, notes of irony sustain through Professor Bloom's remarks: "We all want to find him in the Sonnets, but he is too cunning for us, and you have to be the Devil himself to find Shakespeare there (G. p. 25)." One may suppose this is Dr. Bloom's Freudian Gnostic perspective, considering various critical interpretations of the Sonnets from Francis Meres (classically romantic) through Oscar Wilde (homoeroticism) and so on, saying more about the interpreter than author, which leaves Shakespeare's mysterious implications intact, "circulated among private friends."

In Helen Vendler's book *The Art of Shakespeare's Sonnets* she discounts autobiographical, even Christian nature there and takes issue with essay-like readings for meaning analysis of the Sonnets, by critics like Stephen Booth (p. 13), in favor of pure aesthetic value, while she agrees Sonnet 116 is one of the finest. She spares readers copious metrical analysis, which she quips "would make another book" she feels "not competent to write" as others may like Booth (p. 11) but first offers apologetic wiggle-room: "total emersion in the Sonnets – that is to say, in Shakespeare's mind- is a mildly deranging experience to anyone, and I cannot hope, I suppose, to escape the obsessive features characterizing Shakespearean Sonnet criticism," as if pardoning herself at the outset for any possible arrogance (p. 1).

Dr. Stephen Greenblatt's view, "By keeping his poems at some remove from the actual, Shakespeare was able both to share them intimately... and to circulate them safely among readers," (p. 235) contributes to understanding their personal and potentially dangerous socio-religious political content. A variety of experts claim at length what was or was not essential creation and purpose of *Shakespeare's Sonnets*. Formal elements facilitate ranges of subtle emotion and multiple layers of meaning (Asquith p. 283). Sonnet 29 shows deep anguish, "myself almost despising" and transcendent exaltation, "sings hymns at heaven's gate."

Sonnet 116 takes off on the *Book of Common Prayer*'s marriage vow, "Let me not to the marriage of true minds," recalling psalm-like structure in *New Testament, I Corinthians 13*, and informs, alludes to the list there, of what love is not. He moves into a comedic conceit of the "unknown" value love has as guide for referred-to-ones in: "every wandering bark," "although his height be taken." Transcendent measure of love is ramped up as "not Time's fool." When brief, love can spark endurance "even to the edge of doom." Doubt resolves in a double negative paradoxical hymn-like vow's epiphany, that dares belief in these ideas as error: if wrong he never wrote "nor no man ever loved," which concludes his most profound succinct ode to love as an already highly acclaimed author.

In her book, *Shadowplay: The Hidden Beliefs and Coded Politics of William Shakespeare*, Clare Asquith delves into Sonnet 152's veiled politics: King James I's betrayal of Catholics and the sonnet speaker's patience with an oath of support which self-beguilingly acted as collusion with persecution (p. 285). In terms of "hidden belief" analysis, one could argue outside of the Psalms, the Sonnets are prime examples of early complex coded political and "Confessional Poetics" as a genre or Ars Poetica.

William Wordsworth's deduction of the Sonnets in his own sonnet, "Scorn not the Sonnet," reads: "with this key / Shakespeare unlocked his heart." The Sonnets were discreetly dedicated to Mr. W. H., who one might assume to be the "young man" first addressed in them. The dedication made by publisher Thomas Thorpe (T. T.) did not mean Shakespeare played no part in dedicating, or in the publication as an ordered series, he could have retained discreet background controls in 1609. Professor Greenblatt understands the sonnet "game of love" Shakespeare carefully plays "could lead to the Tower and the scaffold" (p. 234). He presents a possibility that the Sonnets were commissioned and started because he needed money when plague caused theaters to be closed, a time (1592) when he appeared to be transitioning from "successful playwright to cultivated poet" (p. 240-1). Francis Meres in his 1598 book *Wits Treasury,* praised his popular "sugared sonnets among his private friends" and esteemed Shakespeare's "mellifluous honey tongue" with Ovid's "sweet witty soul."

Seeking patronage he wrote *Venus and Adonis* and *The Rape of Lucrece* with dedications to late-teen unmarried Earl of Southampton. Dr. Greenblatt deduces that if the first 126 sonnets "were written to the same person... they sketch a relationship unfolding... over years. Admiration ripens into adoration; periods of joyful intimacy are followed by absence and desperate longing..." (p. 246).

Thorpe's dedication, "To The Onlie Begetter" was like a spin on the Catholic *Apostle's Creed* phrase "only begotten son." The allusion is identified by Yale editor Edward Bliss Reed in his *Notes* section of the 1923 *Shakespeare's Sonnets* facsimile (p. 78) of *The Yale Shakespeare.* Yale published the works of Shakespeare as a same-sized volume set, including the Sonnets. A volume of *Venus and Adonis, Lucrece and the Minor Poems* edited by Albert Feuillerat has extensive notes and appendices. The volume contains *The Passionate Pilgrim* of 1599: 20 poems in two sections, the first contains Shakespeare Sonnets 138 and 144 and two sonnets from the play *Love's Labors Lost*. The second section, *Sonnets to Sundry Notes of Music*, contains a fifth verse poem like a song   not a sonnet from *Love's Labors Lost* IV. iii: 101-120. It is not consistent with sonnet form and a character in the play, Dumaine, refers to it as an ode. This bolsters my understanding of the musical nature of *Shakespeare's Sonnets* in which most recent critical experts seem to gloss over along with the strength of psalm allusions.

Dr. Reed's notes on Sonnet 112. 10, 11. (p. 87): "that my adder's sense to critic and to flatterer stopped are" point to the use of "deaf adder" snake imagery as perhaps oblique allusion to Psalm 58 lines 4 & 5, while using an exact *Coverdale Psalter* quotation: "Even like the deaf adder, that stoppeth her ears; Which refuseth to hear the voice of the charmer, charm he never so wisely." Dr. Stephan Booth's notes (also Yale published) on Sonnet 112's "deaf adder" allusion, uses the *Geneva Bible* quotation rather than Coverdale. He follows with an ironic comment (p. 364): "(Note the expression was traditionally for those who refused to hear truth.)" Dr. Booth's ironic "not hearing truth" due to omissions are noticed by "psalm" and "Coverdale" missing from his index. 50 biblical allusions are indexed at "Bible," 3 psalms are noted, not Psalm 58, referred to in his commentary on Sonnet 112. Dr. Booth makes no mention of the 4 oblique Psalm 17 allusions (I point out later) in Sonnet 17 which also contains the image of "antique song."

The Creed allusion suggests that the "blessing" to Mr. W. H. was on a different level than callow youth, rival poet or rival lover, more like one whose relationship "unfolded over years," resolving in the "sweet nothings" of the last two Sonnets' love myth with a cheeky "all's well that ends well" ending of laughs & smiles to draw a happy curtain on the "154 Sonnets cycle." Love's happy spiritual enterprise is conveyed by the dedication's hope: "All Happiness and that Eternitie Promised by Our Ever-Living Poet," to cover religious and mythical ideals (like proverbial parables) in happiness pursuits of the ever interestingly flawed yet transcendent human. A similar joyous ending exclaims from the final Psalms 149 and 150. Participants are involved with dancing, singing, playing musical instruments while exhorted to make "new" songs of praise to the Lord, conveying an endless expression of redemption praising love as a clear universal ideal (as done by W. S.).

From the first Sonnet's first line to last Sonnet's last, the dedication-fulfilling cycle achieves exponential reinvention effects of an extended crown of sonnets. The first line's universal "we" in "we desire increase" wants the same as plural God, *Genesis* 1:26, who also commands "Increase and multiply" (...new songs and souls? Yes.). An allegorical tease, "little love-god," of the last Sonnet's first line, displays wit for the "fairest creatures" from the first Sonnet, as receiver of that promised "Eternitie" the "alpha and omega" of this Sonnet series -first line to last: "From fairest creatures we desire increase" "Love's fire heats water, water cools not love." Enlightenment, shown in Shakespeare's psychological humorous myth development of desire, seeks to spur (perhaps the dedicatee) on to fulfill pleasant biblical tasks of providing "increase."

Marchette Chute in her charming book, *Shakespeare of London*, quotes Thomas Thorpe's formal dedication: "To the Right Honorable, William, Earl of Pembroke... etc.," that goes on for ten more lines before Thorpe signs, "Your Lordship's humble devoted T. T." Chute's point is Thorpe's dedication of the Sonnets to Mr. W. H. could not have been for a nobleman, only a commoner (p. 343); no mention of Psalms is given other than of King James I, a published author, translating "some of the Psalms," who had written "a study of the *Apocalypse*," "a treatise on demonology," while "having produced a great many poems" and "a book of advice to poets" (p. 253-4). Benson Bobrick (p. 267) concludes that the literary King James I was so weak in other areas of rule that after his death, it resulted in the English civil war, a culmination of conflict between the Crown, Catholics and anti-papist/reformers such as the Puritans.

Wait for more irony. Chute relates "unicorn tales" brought to London from America: "Unicorns were mentioned even in the Bible and it was well known that the horn of the animal, pulverized and boiled in wine, made an excellent mouthwash" (p. 62). This was Chute's extent of biblical allusion commentary, amusing but zilch when it came to Psalm allusions found in Shakespeare's writing. The irony is if she had looked in the Bible for where unicorns are "seen" she could have found Psalm 29 (& 92) where Coverdale's English translated Psalter was set to be sung in church with this pair of lines: "He maketh them also to skip like a calf; / Libanus and Sirion, like a young unicorn."

Close reading reveals key words and conceptual phrases from Myles Coverdale's metrical English Psalms permeate (through direct or oblique allusion) overall structure of the Sonnet series with several Sonnets having same-numbered Psalm allusions. The Sonnets work like a strange ironic mirror, Shakespeare's personal mirror of *Psalms*, *Proverbs*, *The Song of Solomon*, *I Corinthians 13*, etc., all together, no named characters, yet at times individuals (i.e. young man, rival poet, dark lady, etc.) are consecutively implied. This makes the Sonnet cycle a currently alive, perpetual veiled narrative gift, like Shakespeare's secular "psalm-ets" of love (Hotson p. 271-281).

Dr. Leslie Hotson saw allusions in parallel numbered Sonnet and Psalm 107 (with Sonnet 107's Armada crisis background) and 124 (alluding to an assassination plot) (p. 270). Other Sonnets with same-numbered Psalm allusions (6, 32, 51, 102) for Hotson proved Shakespeare's "canonical order of the Sonnets" (p. 280). Sonnet/Psalm allusions in Hotson's notes (p. 281) come from the *Coverdale Psalter* translation (1535) updated later for *The Book of Common Prayer* through Shakespeare's day when "Psalm-singing parishioners included theatre-goers" (p. 272). These Psalms remained in *The Book of Common Prayer* among Catholics and church reformers alike to current times. Hotson also cites Richard Noble's writing, *Shakespeare's Biblical Knowledge* (1935), which indicates there are "some 150 Psalm references from the plays" (p. 272) (same number coincidentally, as Psalms in the Bible).

Hotson points out where in Psalm 6 and Sonnet 6 loss of "beauty" sets tone and image. Then in Psalm and Sonnet 32, image of "my bones" in death sets the tone. Psalm and Sonnet 102 share mournful sound images: a sparrow in the Psalm and Philomel singing in the Sonnet (p. 281). This prompted a search for allusions from other Psalms in corresponding numbered Sonnets. Sonnet 1's first line, mentioned earlier, "From fairest creatures we desire increase" alludes to perhaps the fairest creatures of all, Adam and Eve, and the "increase and multiply" directive. It also obliquely alludes to the image in Psalm 1: "like a tree planted by the water-side that will bring forth his fruit in due season. / His leaf also shall not wither." These allusions add universal implications to the Sonnet.

Sonnets 29, 43 and 116 contain allusions to corresponding numbered Psalms, though some allusions are more oblique than overt. Sonnet 29's theme contends with rising above self-dejection in remembrance of transcendent love that nothing can negate. It takes us from depths of self-loathing, "almost despising," to "sweet love rememb'red" compared to upward flight, as in a new day, away from moody earthbound morass, to "sing hymns at heaven's gate," where he would "scorn to change" his "state with kings." The subtext of Psalm 29 recalls glorious ways the Lord interacts with nature, lands and people, where the Lord is above terrors of flood and remains "a King for ever." In the last lines, "the Lord shall give strength onto his people" and "the blessings of peace" are alluded to in Sonnet 29 by what "such wealth brings."

Sonnet 43's allusion to Psalm 43's: "O send out thy light and thy truth, that they may lead me," is made as the speaker states his "eyes" in dream "are bright in dark directed" "with thy much clearer light" where his "eyes be blessed made," fitting the Psalm's tonal allusion, "that I may go unto the altar of God... the God of my joy and gladness." Redemptive implications are the same in both. The Psalm asks for defense of "my cause against the ungodly people" and for deliverance "from the deceitful and wicked man" while the Sonnet begins with colloquial comedic slang, "when most I wink," as the speaker refers to seeing best in dreams because with awake eyes: "all the day they view things unrespected," which mirrors the Psalm's perception of injustice.

In Psalm 116, "I will pay my vows" is found twice, first followed with "now in the presence of all his people" and a few passages later, "in the sight of all his people," for a   chorus effect. Psalm 116's theme is how the Lord reveals his love through deliverance. Preservation is offered to "the simple" when one in misery hastily exclaims, "All men are liars," yet is heard by the Lord with "the cup of salvation." Remembrance of what the Lord has done for him compels the speaker's devotion to pledge vows of service. Service is oppositely implied by the sonnet speaker's ending, if wrong he "never writ, nor no man ever loved." The overall sense of Sonnet 116 resolves like a series of vows that moves into a sworn "negative" oath at the end.

Religious connotations in Sonnet 29 extend like a "Big Bang" of enlightenment from the compact sonnet form. Shakespeare's crown like extensions and Psalm-mirroring evokes strength and weakness characterizing human condition. Beaut is in the mind's ear, beheld by close readers, loved ones recognizing themselves, interchangeable, revealing extended goals of love, for others as for oneself.

In response to those only seeing "thinness of or lack of pervasive Psalm-mirroring" in the Sonnets, I compared Coverdale's (and the *Geneva*) Psalm 17 to Sonnet 17 that use key words like "heaven." The allusions there, quoting Sonnet then Psalm are: "hides your life / hide me under; beauty of your eyes / apple of an eye; men of less truth than tongue / men, I say, and from the evil world; some child of yours / They have children."

Sonnet 17 also has a good lead-in for a few concluding epiphanies. The poet refers to his "papers" being "scorned" generally and by what is specifically embodied in 17, his inability to accurately describe beauty attributes of the loved one addressed. He gives that future critics would say "this poet lies" with the "stretch`ed miter of an antique song" plying a metrical (and "crown" metaphor?) idea in the line which also lends song-like echo (Help me, Helen Vendler (p. 116) who copies miter as meter as if to correct spelling) to the ending couplet's singing rhyme of time / rime.

Coverdale's Psalms, praised for musicality are used in *Handel's Messiah* and retain their place in the English Psalter of churches throughout England with tweaked adjustments over the years for being sung or read like an English cross-denominational Bible text.

In Shakespeare's play, *Love's Labor's Lost*, Act IV, Scene III, line 157 reads, "Tush, none but minstrels like of sonneting!" To read his Sonnets more deeply one needs to be aware of historical context, family life and socialization in line with his vast literary talents. Music was an important part of his life influenced by religious practice and as an actor/playwright. His Sonnets, like 29, 43 and 116 can be sung as melodiously as any Coverdale Psalm adjusted over the years.

With the concept of Carl Jung's universal pool of the unconscious mind, one could argue that even modern day English pop songs like the Beatles' "Let it Be" (a phrase that came to Sir Paul McCartney in a dream, spoken to him for consolation by his departed mother, as he said after singing it, on James Cordon's *Late Late Show*, "Carpool Karaoke" in Liverpool, June 16, 2018 on the CBS Network) and "Eleanor Rigby," stem from English Psalter tradition, which *Shakespeare's Sonnets* seem to mirror at times and take part in its crowning achievements (as great hymns do like English clergyman John Newton's 1773 "Amazing Grace," sung by President Barak Obama at a memorial service for slain Black Charleston, South Carolina church members).

With this Sonnet cycle Shakespeare reinvented the crown of sonnets by doing away with repetitive last line/first line motifs in favor of conceptual development forms that vary from the traditional crown of seven sonnets. Some scholars like Sir Edmund Chambers and Northrop Frye (Hotson p. 269) see the first 126 as being in Shakespeare's chronological sequence with the following Sonnets possibly arranged by the first publisher (T. T.). Both 126 and 154 are divided evenly by 7. The 154 Sonnets contain 22 crown's worth of sonnets, where the number is closest to the 150 Psalms.

While contemplating scholarly commentary in regard to certain seemingly obvious analytical points pertaining to *Shakespeare's Sonnets*, I glanced at the Jan. 1, 2018 cartoon cover of *The New Yorker* magazine dominated by a huge oblivious grey elephant in a largesketchy living room, standing between a silently seated vexed looking older couple deep in their own annoyed thoughts. The title is: "Cramped" and comes from the hand of cartoonist George Booth, in my imagination somehow related to that heavy lifter of Sonnet commentary, Stephen Booth, whose massive commentary (nearly 450 pgs.) is the "elephant in the room" and needs addressing in terms of my "big picture" understanding of *Shakespeare's Sonnets* as a deliberate operatic epic with peaks, valleys, variations "doing the police in different voices," held together by circular language, codes, allusions, form and metrics.

Sonnet 8 seems to be the closest Dr. Booth gets to the musicality of the whole Sonnet enterprise, a bit ironically as the first line runs, "Music to hear, why hear'st thou music sadly?" In commentary on this (p. 144) he refers to the "serious logical inconsistency" of its "chiasmically balanced epithet and question" echoing exaggerations that then "analyze the inconsistency with inappropriately rigorous logic" through the descending lines of the quatrain (thick irony had here considering Booth's own devises, such is what award winning stuff like his immense book is made of!) he gets the coming "sexual overtones" and parses them handily all the way to the "concord" and "union" of sonnet matrimony. Then following two pages of commentary he lands on an oblique reference to a possible Shakespeare pun attempt used similarly in the play, *All's Well that Ends Well* III.ii.20-22, with a play on words "not, note," with "knot" as what a Renaissance reader may actually have heard!

This leads to his ironic oversight as a near aside to Webster's dictionary: "knot" somehow meaning "ornamental garden," as Booth finds in "...(John) Marston's play *Malcontent*, where Burbadge (theater proprietor, "The Money" buffoon in the film: *Shakespeare in Love*) says (musical) additions introduced into the play are "only as your salad to your great feast, to entertain a little more time, and to abridge the not-received custom of music in our theatre (p. 146)." Here I will leave the elephant's ironically cramped room for wider spaces where arias may be heard in the open air!

The Sonnets accomplish a sublime expression of craft and personal/ universal experience that was best achieved first by the ancient Greeks and "King David's" Psalms which were works known to be sung. David's name is in 6 Psalms. There are tribes and nations but no other contemporaries of David are named. Historical figures are mentioned: Moses, Aaron, Abraham, Isaac, Dathan, Abiram, Phinehas, Melchizedek, Joseph, Jesse and Jacob (mostly, over a dozen times). The only woman found mentioned is in Psalm 51's added intro statement of the 1560 *Geneva Bible* of Shakespeare's time; the Psalm's commentary states it is David's cry for mercy in fallen sinfulness after approached by the prophet Nathan revealing David's sin against and with Bathsheba.

Shakespeare's personal Sonnet "odyssey," like David's, is Homeric and mythic/anti-mythical but with no names though various sonnets sound like different character voices, even female at times, similar to his dramas. Gerald Massey in his 1888 book, *The Secret Drama of*

Shakespeare's Sonnets Unfolded, after offering eloquent investigative evidence like a trial lawyer, points out characters Shakespeare knew and veiled in the Sonnets with their personal traits and dramatic motives. Massey presents a group of Sonnets:

144, 33, 34, 35, 41, 42, 133, 134, 40, in this explicated order (p. 205-10) and goes on to say:

"Elizabeth Vernon's jealousy of her lover the Earl of Southampton and her friend and cousin Lady Rich, is told in these nine sonnets, which are now for the first time put together: they go to Autolycus's tune of "Two Maids Wooing a Man." The first sonnet contains a soliloquy on the subject, a form employed more than once in the dramatic Sonnets. Then we have five Sonnets addressed to the Earl, and three to the lady of whom Elizabeth Vernon is jealous (Lady Rich) (p. 210-11)."

Autolycus, the ballad selling rogue in *The Winter's Tale,* 4.4.310-13, refers to a merry ballad which "...goes to the tune of 'Two Maids Wooing a Man:' there's scarce a maid westward but she sings it; tis in request, I can tell you." Massey seems to know the tune enough to capitalize on it in 1888. By 2017, Catherine Henze in her book *Robert Armin and Shakespeare's Performed Songs,* refers to the song among others also sung by Armin as Autolycus. She notes the lyrics but not the music came down to us (as Autolycus' other song melodies did) (p. 84). In 1599, Armin, also a writer (*Quips for Questions*) was hired as a musician/actor by Shakespeare for the Chamberlain's Men and took on the primary roll of the fool (p.1).

Considering Massey's sonnet list order, 33 with ambiguous heavy allegorical landscape imagery, "glorious morning," then spiritual allusions of "celestial face" and "heaven's sun," sounds like a more fitting soliloquy or overture than144. Line 11 of 33, plays loss off of the allegory in a climactic outburst: "But, out! alack! he was but one hour mine," on to end, "heaven's sun staineth." The list goes on fine through 134, then 144 would return to the allegorical images of 33 as a romantic struggle with "good & bad angels." Lastly, 40 bids for an overwhelming conflict resolution hope with "love" used 10 times!

Clare Asquith in her "Selection of Coded Terms" (p. 299) refers to 33 as alluding to Christ's passion and age of death and the age Shakespeare was when his son Hamnet died, which seems most fitting to bear the grandest allegorical and transcendent soliloquy weight of his Sonnet series.

Regarding the veiled sonnet characters named by Massey, it is compelling to see the Lady Penelope Rich saga Massey lays out, with Sir Philip Sidney's connection (p. 352-6), is also brought out in agreement but with more emphasis on Sidney, by Clare Asquith in 2005's *Shadowplay* (p. 151). Massey compiled such a thorough dossier on Lady Rich's beauty that perhaps even Cleopatra's beauty received less notice by Shakespeare. Massey argues at length that Lady Rich, the first love (though unrequited) of Sir Sidney, was the model for Shakespeare's later Dark Lady sonnets (after #126 and earlier) as well as being Sidney's "chiaroscuro" eyed inspiration for Stella (p. 356). Clare Asquith compiles a similarly weighty analysis of Sir Sidney being the linchpin model/influence for the character and voice of Hamlet from several aspects included in his books: *A Defense of Poesie, Arcadia* and his epic sonnet sequence *Astrophel and Stella*, as well as the facts and legendary points of interest pertaining to his English nobility and death at 32 by an infected thigh wound in a described indecisive/useless action (p. 147-52). Clare Asquith refers to *A Defense of Poetry* as: "...colloquial, graceful, at once casual and learnedly authoritative, in the witty tradition of Erasmus and Montaigne... a bastion of common sense, written in reply to a critic on the theatre..." Lady Rich, according to Asquith, as "the beautiful and intelligent sister of Essex (who was beheaded for treason), an active member of his dissident circle," was one who "...may have been providing acceptable cover for poetry that was in fact political and religious" in aiding Catholics (p.149). Lady Asquith points out Sidney's writings as: "elaborately allegorical, (that) suggest a gradual disillusion with English Protestantism, and a growing sympathy with the plight of Catholicism" (p. 149).

Turning to Sir Sidney's "Petrarchan" sonnet sequence *Astrophel and Stella*, from which allusions may be seen in Hamlet's voice and divided character and in other plays like *Richard III*, the basic idea is found there for a monumental Shakespeare sonnet sequence. Parallels can be found in Sidney's lines: Sonnet 69.7, "Gone is the Winter of my miserie!" calls to mind Richard III's, "Now is the winter of our discontent." Hamlet's echo can be heard in Sidney's Sonnet 68.10: "Labour to kill in me this killing care" and Sonnet 69.14, "No kings be crown'd but they some covenants make."

Music allusions are found in *Astrophel and Stella*: Sonnet 68.6 on Stella: "With voice more fit to wed Amphion's lyre, " for his Muse in Sonnet 70.3-6:

> She oft hath drunk my tears, now hopes to enjoy
>
> Nectar of mirth, since I love's cup do keep
>
> Sonnets be not bound Prentice to annoy;
>
> Trebles sing high, so well as basses deep;

Then 70.9-14 ends with:

> Come then, my Muse, shew thou height of delight
>
> In well raised notes; my pen, the best it may,
>
> Shall paint out joy, though in but black and white.
>
> Cease, eager Muse; peace, pen, for my sake stay,
>
> I give you here my hand for truth of this,
>
> Wise silence is best musicke unto blisse.

Having achieved the romantic equivalence of "rock star" status after death, Sir Sidney's ending verse here even calls to mind Hamlet's fitting epitaph: "The rest is silence" among his "flight of angels."

Without referring to or judging for or against named individuals, *Shakespeare's Sonnets* resonate universally and instrumentally "Catholic" in their structured confessional sounding concepts of emotional themes (variations of love and betrayal). They can be read as parody of grand literature, the English Bible or immense authorial authority gravely ironic in places. Perhaps no greater irony exists anywhere in English literature so sublimely framed, maintained and followed-through. The sequence could be said to work with the same inner mechanics as the "poem unlimited" Shakespeare wrote of in *Hamlet*.

The lyrical structure based on the crown of sonnets form, makes the Sonnets with anonymous characters, potentially one of the greatest modern operas ever conceived had only someone like Mozart lived long enough to find them and compose with an English librettist, something along the combined lines of *Cosi Fan Tutte*, *The Marriage of Figaro*, *The Magic Flute*, *Don Giovanni*, and his *Requiem* of, by and for love.

Works Cited

Asquith, Clare. Shadowplay: The Hidden Beliefs and Coded Politics of William Shakespeare. New York, N. Y.: Public Affairs, 2005. Print.

Bloom, Harold. Genius: A Mosaic of One Hundred Exemplary Creative Minds. New York, N. Y.: Warner Books, 2002. Print.

Bloom, Harold. The Anatomy of Influence: Literature as a Way of Life. New Haven, Conn.: Yale UP, 2011. Print.

Bobrick, Benson. Wide as the Waters: The Story of the English Bible and the Revolution It Inspired. New York, N. Y.: Simon & Schuster, 2001. Print.

Booth, Stephen. –ed. Shakespeare's Sonnets. New Haven, Conn.: Yale UP, 1977. Print.

Chute, Marchette. Shakespeare of London. N. Y., N. Y.: E. P. Dutton Co., 1949. Print.

Coverdale, Myles. Coverdale's Psalter. San Bernardino, CA: Walter Pub. 2016. Print.

Greenblatt, Stephen. Will in the World: How Shakespeare became Shakespeare. New York, N. Y.: W. W. Norton & Co., 2004. Print.

Henze, Catherine A. Robert Armin and Shakespeare's Performed Songs. N. Y., N. Y. Routledge, 2017. Print.

Hotson, Leslie. Mr. W. H. London: Rupert Hart-Davis, 1964. Print.

Massey, Gerald. The Secret Drama of Shakespeare's Sonnets Unfolded. London, Spottiswoode and Co., 1888. Print.

Reed, Edward Bliss. The Yale Shakespeare: Shakespeare's Sonnets. New Haven, Conn.: Yale UP, 1923. Print.

Schneible, Ann. Was Shakespeare a Secret Catholic? Rome, Italy: CAN/EWTN News, 2016. Web. 20 June, 2016.

Swift, Daniel. Shakespeare's Common Prayers. N. Y., N. Y.: Oxford UP, 2013. Print.

Vendler, Helen. The Art of Shakespeare's Sonnets. Cambridge: Harvard UP, 1999. Print.

Afterword

The 2016 essay on his Sonnets, in the appendix, marked the 400 year death anniversary of Shakespeare and caused reimagining this text as a more thorough tribute. Tulane University professor and Louisiana State Poet Laureate, Peter Cooley, hosted the Sonnet part of a month long series of anniversary events called "First Folio!" The 2016 elaborate production featured readings, recitals, plays, displays of period publications of plays, poems, the Sonnets and an actual *First Folio* opened to *Hamlet* under a Plexiglas cube in Tulane's newly established Newcomb Art Museum.

My trilogy tribute idea with allusions emerged after the essay research. One volume combining the essay and the 3 separate volumes seemed a worthy tribute at 300 sonnets (a number advised 5 years earlier to round the contents down to, from approximately twice that, prior to the essay, by a poet/editor/teacher friend). Reading the essay one can see where my allusion idea came from and what motivations Shakespeare may have had in allusion usage considering the importance of English Bible translations. All Coverdale's translated 150 Psalms in *The Book of Psalms* are also in England's *Book of Common Prayer*.

Many scholars say Shakespeare's allusion choices spread personal, romantic, historical, allegorical, spiritual and philosophical enrichments throughout his work. A more recent young scholar, Daniel Swift in his 2013 Oxford University Press book, *Shakespeare's Common Prayers The Book of Common Prayer and the Elizabethan Age*, for 280 plus pages examines how influential the BCP was on Shakespeare's life and work. When referring to Sonnet 23 (p. 78) he states generally: "The sonnets are games of form and articulation: they are about what truth may be boxed in set speech. Here the truest speaker is an actor, straining for the words of his role." Soon (p. 79) Swift transitions to the Sonnet embodied in Romeo and Juliet's dialogue, "upon meeting" they "speak instantly of holiness" as if a direct embodiment of the prayer book's influence:

ROMEO: If I profane with my unworthiest hand

        This holy shrine, the gentler sin is this:

        My lips, two blushing pilgrims, ready stand

        To smooth that rough touch with a tender kiss.

JULIET: Good pilgrim, you do wrong your hand too much,

        Which mannerly devotion shows in this.

        For saints have hands that pilgrims' hands too touch,

        And palm to palm is holy palmers' kiss.

ROMEO: Have not saints lips, and holy palmers, too?

JULIET: Ay, pilgrim, lips that they must use in prayer.

ROMEO: O then, dear saint, let lips do what hands do:

        They pray; grant thou, lest faith turn to despair.

JULIET: Saints do not move, though grant for prayers' sake.

ROMEO: Then move not while my prayer's effect I take. (1.5.90-103)

An interesting relative passage is found in Harold Bloom's, *A Map of Misreading*, (p. 67) that refers to Milton's "power of religious phenomenology:"

"As a man, evidently he was Christian (of his own sect, a sect of one) but as poet he was a fierce Miltonist, and as much a son of himself as of God. If the Imagination, in poetry, speaks of itself, then it speaks of origins, of the archaic, of the primal, and above all of self-preservation."

Next examining Vico's "magic formalism" used as a tool of the "self-defining function of imagination," Dr. Bloom refers to Auerbach's summary: "The aim of primitive imagination... is not liberty but... establishment of fixed limits, as a psychological and material protection against the chaos of the surrounding world." Thank you Dr. Bloom, several of these aspects mentioned in both passages resonate throughout *Shakespeare's Sonnets* as well as the general structure and purpose of this trilogy.

The formal high modern English with which Shakespeare was well acquainted to the point of being dramatically responsible for its vocabulary expansion through his writing, was based on a good grounding in the holy scriptures, mythology and readings throughout the liberal arts, in law as well as good grammar and Latin education. My own research over the years in a liberal arts education, masters degree in counseling, masters studies in art history, and creative writing as part of an MFA curriculum in poetry and independent studies in the English Bible, immersion in documentary films repeated regularly on cable's History Channel, YouTube videos and the PBS television network, have added to the development of comprehension skills that assisted in propelling me to achieve these poetic works and enlightened thoughts.

Though the title, *Shakespeare AI*, may be a misnomer, it is a catchy "iconcurchaic" one that may afford some stimulation to the poetic memory banks in order to purchase its license worth of parody as well as profundity. One of the bravest challenge pursuits was to include the allusions throughout the trilogy which required a complete revision of the text. Because of the allusion process the work takes on an even more profound aspect of an "artificial Shakespeare intelligence" which is how the title transformation into *Shakespeare AI*, was justified. This title was lastly and strangely aided and abetted by a curious essay in *The Atlantic* magazine, "How the Enlightenment Ends: Philosophically, intellectually –in every way –human society is unprepared for the rise of artificial intelligence" by Dr. Henry A. Kissinger (*The Atlantic*, June 2018). The cover headline refers to it as: *AI and the End of Human History* (quite an opposite bookend to Dr. Harold Bloom's published concept of: *Shakespeare: the Invention of the Human*!)

The title *Shakespeare's Wake*, chosen for volume one, came from one of Dr. Harold Bloom's descriptions of James Joyce's *Finnegans Wake (A. of I.*, p. 112). In the concluding poem, *ASAP*, (last sonnet written for this trilogy) some key words were also inspired by Dr. Bloom, from passages in his 1996 book on "The Gnosis of Angels, Dreams, and Resurrection," *Omens of Millennium*. It is interesting to note that I had not read enough of the book for it to consciously influence the writing of the trilogy before its final poem. I was excited to find several correlations in our use of words and ideas while recently reading his book more deeply, I will return to it. A current version of the poem *ASAP* uses the words: "archon" and "Pleroma" from his splendorous book (p. 239-40).

The term "iconcurchaic" is my invention that is a tribute to the Parisian poet/critic (friend of Picasso) G. Apollinaire, as well as the Bard. The word means something iconic and current while also being archaic, with an implication of timelessness. I hope this book imparts the same to the reader, in various ways not excluding irony, as well as an enriched interest in Shakespeare's work and methods which may lend some forbearance of judgment for readers against the strangeness of my book, who can not read it with the "negative capability" of Keats in mind (of which in a letter Keats wrote: "Shakespeare possessed enormously"). Though this book at times resembles curious best seller oddities such as Calvin Parker's 2018 book, *Pascagoula- The Closest Encounter: My Story*, about his and Charles Hickson's night fishing trip alien abduction experience in 1973, my efforts are validated by pieces on the current Pirate's Alley, Rosemary James and Joseph DeSalvo produced, Faulkner-Wisdom literary contest finalist and short lists.

To bear the Bard's all-encompassing insight toward Horatio's "wondrous strange!" remark upon the interaction of the men with Hamlet's father's ghost, he has Hamlet say:

And therefore as a stranger give it welcome.

There are more things in heaven and earth, Horatio,

Than are dreamt of in our philosophy. But come,

Here as before, never, so help you mercy,

How strange or odd soe'er I bear myself-

As I perchance hereafter shall think meet

to put an antic disposition on-

That you at such time seeing me never shall,

With arms encumbered thus, or this headshake,

Or by pronouncing of some doubtful phrase

As 'Well, we know' or 'We could an 'if we would',

Or 'If we list to speak', or 'There be an 'if they might',

Or such ambiguous giving out, to note

That you know aught of me- this not to do,

So grace and mercy at your most need help you, swear.

GHOST: (*under the stage*) Swear.

    [*They swear*] (1.5.167-182)

During my conversation on copyright for the book with a helpful "tech support" person, Lorraine, at the copyright office, I was told the word "iconcurchaic" should now be placed "in the dictionary" ...certainly, I would feel deeply honored by this and thanked Lorraine while we both chuckled about it.

The artist Lin Emery gave the three book effort a thrilling statement (extracted from here) pertaining to my use of her sublime metaphorical sculpture "Flight" in the composite photographs for the covers of the trilogy *Shakespeare AI* and Vol. 2, *Recycling the Circle*, when emailing after an hour meditation session with the Dali Lama's personal physician: "Your overwhelming poems were a fitting coda... Thank you for including me in your Circles!" What an exquisitely gracious "Zen-engineering artist" she is of the spirit as well as metal!

In 2000 I dreamed of her sculpture "Flight" being on the column instead of Lee at Lee Circle in New Orleans. "Flight" once stood in a perfectly proportioned reflecting pool with exquisite lily pads, lotuses and goldfish, to grace the front of the Museum of Art, a favorite New Orleans structure and setting. I regard it as the museum façade's crowning sculpture that has unfortunately been removed to the shadowy realms of the museum's rearwards "sculpture garden" like a UFO landing in a manicured swamp. The dream inspired my photographic "odd-yssey" in 2000 in which I attempted to "double expose" her sculpture onto the top of the Lee Circle column with 35mm film in an "auto-everything" Nikon camera. It resulted in the 2016 *Recycling the Circle* cover idea, with a framed print of it presented to Mayor Mitch Landrieu (at his 2018 book signing of, *In the Shadow of Statues*) to which he remarked "That's beautiful!" I then mentioned my dream of Lin's sculpture on Lee's column and thought it could then be called Lin Emery Circle. Though he had removed the statue for a more appropriate setting such as cemetery or museum, he said renaming it was not for him to decide. Lin's deep reflections will remain greatly appreciated as this book enters the wider world with care and hopes that it will help enrich lives of readers with a deeper appreciation of *Shakespeare's Sonnets* dedication on behalf of the Bard's "promised eternity," proclaimed to delighted open minds.

M. D. V. 8/17/2018

213

Epithalamic Epilogue & Epitaph

To loving critics who work behind me, beside me or who merely love from distance, themselves as wedded well, but may not know how "good," or those who expect me at the altar of ego or no-go (when what I have is difficult enough to marry without the eternal bridegroom's betrothal), for them this consolation prize. To critics who weigh me in their scales of learned ignorance more blind than the flip side of justice to their own blindness, thin kings of my flittering hybrid's fat stunted imagination, I dedicate to their degrees of "word zymurgy maya" what could have been thoughts of Hamlet to detractors had he survived (as he does here), here's to cool pomposity the parting shot of Sonnet 121:

'Tis better to be vile than vile esteemed,
When not to be receives reproach of being;
And the just pleasure lost, which is so deemed
Not by our feeling, but by others' seeing:
For why should others' false adulterate eyes
Give salutation to my sportive blood?
Or on my frailties why are frailer spies,
Which in their wills count bad what I think good?
No, I am that I am, and they that level
At my abuses reckon up their own:
I may be straight though they themselves be bevel;
By their rank thoughts my deeds must not be shown;
Unless this general evil they maintain,
All men are bad and in their badness reign.

Besides a Psalm (Coverdale's 116: "All men are liars"), this also calls to mind Hamlet's concluding remarks on actor treatment: "better have a bad epitaph than their ill report while you live" (2.2.528-9). So here is an epitaph now:

My ardent spirits do not desert me for fear,
to drink from the bridal glass or last supper cup,
my book's feast serves both scholar and common reader,
may it serve you well with both hands to follow up.

215

www.ingramcontent.com/pod-product-compliance
Lightning Source LLC
Chambersburg PA
CBHW030314180626
46810CB00003B/1072